LIVING & LOVING LIFE ALL DAY EVERY DAY

A MOTHER'S STORY OF LOSS, LOVE AND CONNECTING WITH THE AFTERLIFE

~DIANE CALDERON~

ISBN-13: 979-8-218-23429-4

Library of Congress Control Number-2023914985

Printed in U.S.A.

This book is available at quantity discounts for bulk purchases.

For information, please contact www.DianeCalderon.com

DEDICATION

This book is dedicated to my son Matthew.
Without him this journey would never have begun.
Furthermore, I honor all of those who know the loss of
a child.
No one wants to take this road, but here we are.

Contents

FOREWORD

I believe that there is a reason you are perusing this book at this moment. In fact, this may be a sign from the universe that you are having a wake-up call. Perhaps you are ready to better understand who you truly are as a soul and why you are here on Earth currently.

Let me ask you a question: Have you ever wondered why life is often difficult and seemingly unfair? If you or someone you love is experiencing overwhelming challenges such as grief, then *Living & Loving Life* is a must-read book.

Diane Calderon has provided a roadmap for navigating the ups and downs of your life and integrating your diverse experiences to create your own brand of inner wisdom. She leads us to a beautiful spiritual place by her example. This is an unflinching account of the separate tragic deaths of her husband and adult son and what happens next in her existence.

We feel her processing her emotions, and we take joy in her gaining a profound spiritual connection that leads her to a new adventure.

I know a thing or two about grief, hope, and signs from spirit. As a scientifically verified evidential medium, I have spoken with thousands of people who were grieving the death of a beloved person or pet. My greatest hope is that all who grieve are able to process their emotions in their own unique ways and receive comfort, including direct signs from their loved ones who now live in the spirit world. I am also the evidential medium whom the author meets towards the end of the book. As a postscript to this book, over the years, I mentored and certified Diane as one of only five certified evidential mediums who bear my stamp of approval.

None of us will escape the experience of grief. Although the subject matter is weighty, this book is written in a style and voice that is at once uplifting and engaging. You will not find a slog through sadness here! In fact, *Living & Loving Life* is quite therapeutic. If you are longing to live your life with more inner peace and greater optimism for tomorrow, then read on!

As you accompany Diane on her journey, you may find yourself gently beginning to process your emotions around loss and grief in the manner that is right for you. Or you may simply mine a few golden nuggets of truth that will help you or someone you love. Either way, I know that you will enjoy this helpful, hopeful, and healing true story from someone I deeply admire.

- Susanne J. Wilson, MA – The Carefree Medium & Intuition Educator; Author, *Soul Smart: What the Dead Teach Us About Spirit Communication.* May 2023, Carefree, Arizona, USA.

DANGER AHEAD

One memorable December day, my husband Sal and I exited a medical complex after a follow-up visit with a neurologist. Sal had been previously diagnosed with Lewy Body Dementia, and his prognosis detailed how the disease would progress, as batches of symptoms would bring about a steady decline in cognition and memory issues.

Though he seemed alert enough at times, certain incidents happened in which Sal would hallucinate and react to whatever fantasy had suddenly factored into his level of awareness. As time went on, regular visits to the doctor only led to more concerns.

On this day Sal was doing better than usual. Such moments were becoming increasingly rare, so it was nice to spend time with him when he felt well.

As we headed out of the medical building and approached our car, we were surprised by the presence of our son, Matthew, leaning against our vehicle with a big smile and a pleasant "hello." The day before, I had shared with him that we would be in Phoenix for Sal's current appointment and hoped to stop by his house for a quick visit.

Matthew thought he could catch us at the medical center in time for a quick lunch before we headed back to our home in northern Arizona. When we met, each one of us exchanged hugs. Always happy to engage with Matthew, we looked forward to hanging out with him at a local diner.

During lunch over burgers and fries, Matthew shared some stories about his current job. He had been working for several months as a remodeler on a renovation project at the airport. My son had always been a good storyteller; we could not help but laugh along with him as he relayed humorous incidents from working with a mixed group of fellow remodelers.

After a few laughs, we finished our meal and headed back home. Although we lived a couple of hours away, the drive always seemed to take a bit longer each time we left the Phoenix area.

Matthew mentioned there were some things he wanted us to pick up at his home before we left the area. As his house was along our travel route, we agreed to stop by and pick up the items as he requested.

Matthew's home represented a project we had agreed to engage in a few years earlier. The house was one of those in need of major renovations when he stumbled onto it during a hiatus in the fluctuating real estate market. Since we were able to purchase the property, Matthew agreed to do the remodeling and all the upgrade work. There was the expectation that, at some point, we would sell it and each of us would make a nice, tidy profit. All told, the undertaking was not a bad business deal. Meanwhile, though, Matthew was slow to finish the project.

Tempted to find work here, there, and everywhere, Matthew often found his energies directed away from the main task at hand. Fortunately for everyone involved, we turned out to be very patient investors.

Several minutes after departing from the restaurant, I turned the car onto 23rd Avenue, one of those quiet tree-lined feeder streets found in the Phoenix area. Matthew's home was just a few short blocks ahead in a nice, quiet neighborhood of homes built in the 50's and 60's. The area was a bit like a step back in time, with older block homes, neatly trimmed yards, and established trees.

Where we were headed was not a heavily traveled district. Only one lane ran through a residential area, a community lined with a couple of schools, some small churches, as well as an adjoining neighborhood park.

Driving up 23rd, being cautious to not exceed the speed limit, I noticed there was almost no sign of traffic that afternoon. School was in session, which may have explained why I didn't see anybody hanging out at the local park as we approached the turn towards Matthew's home.

Suddenly Sal screamed, "Stop! Stop! Stop!" Startled, I slammed on the brakes and came to an abrupt stop in the middle of the road. Sal was clawing at the dashboard and pumping his foot down on the floor as if he had been the one driving the car, compelled to hit the brakes to avoid slamming into a phantom pedestrian crossing the road.

Sal was frantic. "He is going to get hit!" he yelled. I explained to Sal there was absolutely no one ahead of us, and that there was nobody around who could possibly get hit. "No, no, no you have to stop!" Sal insisted. He was intent that I follow his warning. I did as he asked. I was too frightened to do anything else.

So, I eased the car over towards the bicycle path, shifted to neutral, and tried to calm Sal down. During our recent trips together, this was not the first time that Sal had gotten so upset; at this point, he was almost completely out of hand.

A few months prior, there had been a frightening incident during our travels. On that occasion, Sal thought he was being kidnapped and tried to jump out of the car as I was driving down the freeway.

While struggling to keep control of the vehicle, I clutched at Sal's arm and tried to calm him down. At this point, he was actively trying to open his door to escape an unknown assailant who existed only in his mind. In my shock and fear, I managed to reason that I needed help. I knew something else had to happen, something unexpected and even more life changing. Clearly, Sal seemed frightened of me, his own wife. I had little or no choice but to pull off the road and make a quick call to the sheriff's office. Fortunately, a kind deputy soon arrived. The deputy was able to ease Sal's fears; she even offered to give him a ride home. Thankfully, Sal felt safer with the deputy, and was more than happy to escape from me. Whatever fears he had flowing through his mind, the deputy had offered an easy solution. As he settled into the sheriff's vehicle for a ride home, I was more than a little grateful and plainly relieved.

All in all, Lewy Body Dementia had a way of popping up unexpectedly; in truth, at times it was accompanied by some very bizarre side effects: One never knew what was going to happen and why. I felt like Sal was on a roller coaster. Sometimes he was fine, and then he would dip down into some horrible place where he was lost, confused, and scared. Often, incidents would appear that tested my patience and abilities to calm him. On each occasion, all I wanted was to arrive safely at home without either of us getting hurt.

Those experiences taught me to take Sal seriously whenever a crazy bout of paranoic fantasy showed any sign of erupting and bubbling out of nowhere. Whenever any of these episodes occurred, I had to use my words, carefully and sparingly. Today was no different. In the face of the present moment, I recalled the earlier episodes. Now, I didn't quite know what to do.

Trying to calm his fears I calmly said, "No one else is on the road, Sal, so no one is going to get hurt. It's all going to be okay."

He disagreed and snapped back, "No, you almost hit that man, didn't you see him? This is a very dangerous road. Someone is going to get hurt. Don't drive here. Use a different road."

Exasperated, I gave in: "Okay, let's get off this street. We will go straight home, and no one will get hurt."

These last words seemed to ease his anxiety. I pulled up to the next side street, turned and headed towards the freeway. Whatever Matthew wanted us to pick up could wait. Two hours later, I pulled into our driveway, relieved that no other outbursts or fears from Sal had erupted during the otherwise uneventful ride home.

Matthew called later to ask why we hadn't stopped to pick up the boxes he had put together for us. I recounted the situation with Sal. I was truly concerned about his outburst. For reasons known only to him, Sal did not want me to drive down that particular road leading to the house. He was convinced that someone was in harm's way, and I had to get off the street. That is why I agreed to turn around and come straight home using a different and less familiar street. Thank God, there had been no other incidents!

Matthew responded to the whole situation in this way: "Mom, I'm getting worried that something bad is going to happen. How many times has Pops tried to get out of the car when you are driving? He seems to be getting worse, and I am wondering what we should do about all this. Maybe you need to stop bringing Pops to Phoenix. Maybe you can find another doctor closer to home. I don't want you or him to ever get hurt."

I knew Matthew was right to be concerned. Sal was declining; it was all happening in fits and starts, as the saying goes. He had long periods where he appeared relatively normal, but, unfortunately, many new episodes were occurring, ones marked by anxiety and fear.

Intense fear at times! These concerning outbursts had appeared increasingly challenging as time moved forward. Matthew was right; I needed to stop making the long drives to Phoenix. I needed to get Sal set up with some reliable and local medical help. It was time to make major decisions; with a new year fast approaching, other changes might be in the offing. Though I was more than ready to make new arrangements, somehow, I felt I was not acting as quickly as I should. I just needed a little more time to make those important adjustments.

"LEWY"

Two weeks after the outlandish scare with Sal during the drive home, we entered a New Year—hello 2014! Normally I would enter the start of the year with hopes for prosperity, great health, good times—the usual when we raise a toast to the year to come. This year though, things did not look so wonderful.

It had been three years since Sal had experienced a mini stroke when a TIA (transient ischemic attack) struck, unexpectedly. This setback came out of nowhere. Sal was still a rather strong, healthy, active man. He rarely slowed down, always finding something to do: gardening, yard work, handyman projects, reading and enjoying life. He was in really good shape for a retiree. A mini stroke caught us off guard.

In time, this TIA seemed to have been the trigger point, a moment when Sal began the slow decline, physically and mentally. One year following the first episode, he was getting worse, depressed, and having difficulties with simple tasks and comprehension. A neurologist diagnosed early stages of Lewy Body Dementia, bluntly stating there was no cure, and little medication that could help. We were devastated.

Shocked and uninformed about dementia, especially the Lewy Body version, I began to search for insights, answers, and understanding as to what was in store with this diagnosis. What I found did not alleviate my worries: We were in for a rough ride.

Lewy Body Dementia had no cure, no easy drug or fix to extend one's life and help with memory and delusions. By early 2014, Lewy Body Dementia became that uninvited guest in our home and refused to leave Sal alone. "Lewy", as I began to label the situation, had settled into our lives, and there was no way out of that calamity. Sal was on the road to leaving this physical world, sooner than I had hoped, and Lewy was helping him along.

Episodes of Sal being lost or not recognizing me or trying to go back home to Mexico to be with his mom were becoming our new norm. He could be fine for a few days, almost like Lewy had gone on a vacation. Those periods of quiet were becoming less frequent, but most welcome when they were happening.

Then there were the increasingly challenging events, coming more frequently. These episodes could be quite difficult and unpredictable. One day Sal could be sweet talking, flirting with me. *Nice*—except the name he used was not mine. Maybe a girlfriend from his past? That was a bit unnerving.

Another day he'd avoid me like the plague, as if I was out to hurt him. Once I was working on our taxes. Sal came up and grabbed the papers on the table and would not give them back. I asked, "What are doing?" and he replied, "I know you are stealing from me, these are mine." He walked away, papers clutched tightly in his hand, refusing to give them over. I retrieved them later, when he dozed off, a tight grip on those "stolen documents."

I will never forget the afternoon when a viral bug was hitting me, a crummy feeling that would not subside. I just wanted to take some medicine and lay down for a little while, and maybe get up feeling a little bit better. Sal said he was fine, just sitting in the recliner watching some nature documentary. I headed to the bedroom, lay down, and dozed off.

Thirty minutes later, I was abruptly awakened to Sal, standing in the doorway, yelling at me. "I saw him!" he shouted, angry and ready to fight. Groggy and not quite sure what was in his mind, why the sudden anger, I asked "Who?"

Sal replied in a jealous rage, "Your boyfriend! He just ran out of the room! He was in here with you, I knew something was wrong and came to find him in bed with you!" *Oh boy*. I did not see that coming. There had never been any reason for him to go off into that hallucination, but there it was. I made sure to never try and take another afternoon nap after that incident.

On two occasions Sal took off, bolted out the door, headed down the driveway and out the gate, as fast as his legs would take him. Fortunately, on both adventures to escape,

Matthew was visiting and able to jump in the car and do a search and rescue before Sal reached the dangerous highway a mile down the road. Matthew would catch up to him, and ask "Hey Pops, where are you going? Need a ride?" Sal would respond, "I am going to the bus stop, I need to go home." At least Sal felt safe with Matthew and would follow his directions to get in the car and return home safe and sound.

My worries that Sal may slip out again, head to the highway, and meet a tragic ending led me to start locking the gate at the end of the drive, hoping that would stop him from any further journeys to the non-existent bus stop. When Sal was outside, I watched him like a hawk. Though the fencing around the property was four feet high, he could be anxious enough to find a way over. When Matthew was not around, I was especially diligent, as another escape could have disastrous consequences.

Weeks earlier, Sal's bizarre emotional reaction that unfolded so dramatically as I drove down the street towards Matthew's house, worried me. I did not know if Sal's anxieties that day were stemming from some inner sense of knowing, some place he'd hidden in his mind about where he might be heading. Did he harbor a general fear he'd always possessed regarding the act of dying? Perhaps, that was it! Doubtless, more incidents were fated to come—more hallucinations and more reactions.

All in all, such episodes could make life with Lewy Body Dementia even more challenging. I did not know what to expect, nor how much I could take moving forward. More than once I would daydream a fantasy, an escape, to just leave and not look back, but my heart would and could not do that. I just needed a little respite, now and then, away from Lewy and the growing worries.

My commitment to care for Sal was leading me deeper into a new reality. Being engaged in a deeper caregiving phase was drawing me down and draining my energy. My support for help was very limited as we lived in a rural locale. Only a handful of friends, none of whom lived in the immediate area, were close by. My brother and a stepson lived within 30 minutes of our home; despite that short distance, both had health issues to contend with. All in all, they were not in the best shape to assume a supportive caretaker role.

Matthew was my best bet and my best helper, yet he lived all of two hours away. In any event, whenever I needed him, he always came. Otherwise, I was on my own. Taking care of Sal was my prime responsibility and that was that.

Before Lewy moved in, Sal had been a wonderful husband. He loved holding hands, dancing, reading, and watching movies; he was a kind and generous man; enjoyed people and children and dogs and so much of life. I was fortunate to share that life with him, too.

Those memories carried me in the moments I would see him lost and confused. I would wonder if he felt joy in this new version of life now. I could never be completely sure exactly what he felt or sensed. Where had his soul flown? Where was Sal?

While I could not predict the details of what was to

come our way, I could not deny that I fostered many questions. How bad will life with this disease be? Would Sal get worse, and need to be placed in a care home indefinitely? Could we afford the costs of that kind of care? Did he have months or years to live out the effects of this horrible disease of "Lewy" dementia? How could I know? I often wondered: did I really have the skills and the wherewithal to manage these challenges? At least I was retired and healthy and able to care for Sal, for a while. Nonetheless, I did not want to start the New Year even beginning to think in these very cold and yet, all too necessary, practical terms.

MY SON

Early in the new year, Matthew came to visit us for a few days. His latest job had ended; he was looking for a new direction. At 35 years old he was no longer satisfied with working for others and wanted to fulfill his long-held passion with a major career commitment.

During most of his young life, Matthew nourished dreams of becoming a building contractor. Sal had introduced him at the tender age of 10 to the world of home building. We had purchased several acres in rural Arizona, north of Prescott, with plans to build our retirement home.

Building this house, with some help from friends and relatives, was an experience. We would drive up from Phoenix whenever the weather was decent to work on every aspect of the project. Matthew was usually at Sal's side, learning how to install pipes and electrical wiring, pour a foundation, frame the walls, insulate, drywall, texture, and paint, and so forth and so on. My job was to help, run to town for materials and occasional lunches, and assist as well as I could. Construction was not my thing, but I enjoyed seeing our dream home take shape.

It took five years of planning, designing, and construction from the ground up, most of this done on weekends. By the time Matthew entered high school we had built our home and moved in. I remember he did balk a little at the idea of leaving his big city urban high school in the Phoenix area for the small, rather not so hip school in town.

"Mom, I do not want to get 'hick-tified.' Can't I just stay down here and finish high school? I can stay with someone and not have to hang out with those cowboys and hicks." *Oh, sure Matthew.*

Well, we caved in, knowing that would not last long. Sure enough, after three weeks away from us, Matthew was willing to do anything to get back home, where the heart is. No doubt he missed my home cooking, and over time, some of those "hicks" became his best friends.

Constructing a house was such a fun project that we decided to build another one. Sal was retired, and I had not yet looked for a job, so we had time on our hands. We split our acreage and engaged in another home construction. *Why not?* We had the skills and the time, and we could make a nice profit when it sold. This one went much quicker; Matthew was older and able to do so much more. Plus, we lived next door, so no more long weekends of driving up from Phoenix.

Matthew enjoyed all aspects of building, so much so

that after graduating from high school, he enrolled in Construction Management courses at the local community college. One day he came home with a proposal. For course credits, he could design a home. He asked if we would be willing to go one step further, hire him to build this home and fund the construction—another project to build and sell, make a few bucks. After some discussion and financial finagling, Matthew's project became a reality. He designed, and built, a very attractive home. Sal and I helped with the construction—well, more Sal than I. This really became a father and son type of project.

Matthew's passion for creating and constructing homes led him to a variety of jobs in the field. He worked for several contractors, builders, remodelers, even maintenance jobs for the next few years. He supervised one large residential project that involved designing and renovating. It gave him a taste of what a career as a contractor could lead to, and he hoped to someday follow through and get licensed to do just that.

In between the jobs in construction, he had to find other avenues of revenue to get by. He worked as a supervisor's assistant at a Nevada gold mining operation one year. During another period, he worked for a major oil drilling company, as a cementer, in Colorado and Wyoming. He spent a summer in Colorado as a river raft guide, and performed a variety of short-term jobs as a waiter in the hospitality business, as well as side jobs for friends who wanted to add a room addition here, build a sunroom there, create a beautiful staircase, maybe roof someone's home or put up a fence—anything reasonable to keep busy and pay the bills.

After all these years, Matthew at the age of 35, had finally decided it was time to follow through with his dreams and get serious. "Mom, I am tired of working here and there and never getting anywhere solid. I am going to buckle down and take the contractor's exam. I want to start my own company. Can you help me?"

Of course! I planned to help as much as I could. Every parent dreams of the day their child wants to get serious with life, and settle into a good career. Finally, it looked like that day was just around the corner. *Yay*!

Matthew was already familiar with most of the rules for construction licensing, having studied the professional aspects in his college days. With a refresher course, he felt he was almost ready to pass his exams without too much trouble. His only weakness lay in all the busy paperwork, as well as the various legal procedures associated with the managerial exam requirements.

Regarding these administrative requirements, Matthew and I made a very practical agreement: I would attend to the business side of things; on his part, he would contribute by standing in as the professional builder. It helped that much of my prior work experience had been in government, working on contracts, budgets, and lots of administrative paperwork. I could dive into the business aspect without too much trouble. All in all, we would collaborate on the business plans, and we expected we would be very successful.

Initiating a new venture with my son gave me a much-needed boost. The prospect of developing a little company, maybe assisting after things were established with office tasks, phone calls with potential clients, and keeping Matthew on task was a bit exciting. A brighter future, in at least this area of my life, was possible! For both of us!

Caregiving for Sal would take more of my time in the coming months, but I was confident there would be ample opportunities to focus on this adventure. I was excited with a renewed purpose in my life, one that could lead to something later, after Sal was no longer needing my care. All in all, it would be great to see Matthew finally move forward with his dreams as well.

Matthew and I began working towards our new goal. He would brush up on his knowledge of rules, regulations, details on construction; meanwhile, I started researching the administrative requirements: preparing taxes, filing with state agencies to do business, setting up accounts, and establishing a name for the company. Matthew was the muscle; I was the smarts, so to speak.

I took advantage of Matthew being around those chilly January days. Planning and studying for the business did not take all our time. Not only did I get him to take care of a few handyman type projects, but I engaged him in some good conversations, discussions which I had been sorely lacking in my life in recent months. In better days, Sal and I used to discuss a lot of topics, from politics to religion, stories and movies, and so much more, but his dementia was pulling him to a different world, and those conversations were few and further away as time moved forward. I took advantage of having another person in the house to talk to, and Matthew loved to talk, a lot. He was always a chatty person, with strong opinions on several subjects. We did not always agree on major points, but it was fun to interact and learn from his point of view.

One subject at the forefront of my mind pertained to the seriousness of Sal's deteriorating condition. Matthew had witnessed a few of the scary incidents with his Pops. Many episodes had played out over the previous year. Most of the time, however, Matt had not been around for many of the daily challenges.

I had noticed that often, when Matthew would visit for a short period, Sal would be on his best behavior. He saved his more anxious and paranoid moments for when no one was around, except me. When I would share some of my experiences regarding Sal's behaviors, I wondered if Matthew sometimes thought I was making up stories, as he rarely saw Sal in his Lewy costume when he was around.

Staying at the house with us over the course of several days allowed Matthew to experience some of what I had been sharing. Sal could not wear his disguise of good behavior for too long, and eventually his paranoia and anxieties emerged. Matthew was a bit shaken by some of the little outbursts.

Almost every morning, Sal needed help getting bathed and dressed. At times, his eyes would tear up so much that he had trouble seeing. His interest in normal life was waning. I could not deny there were still times when he could understand what was going on around him. Sometimes, Sal was able to fully engage in rounds of social conversation.

Otherwise, there were periods when Sal seemed to exit the planet; often, he appeared to engage in a regular practice of doing just that, his mind floating off into another world. That development seemed to take Matthew by surprise.

More shocking were the accusations. One afternoon Sal started getting upset with Matthew and told him to get out of the house. "I don't want you here, you are no good, a bum, a druggie. Get out!" Sal yelled, pointing towards the door. There was no precursor to this, no rhyme nor reason. Somewhere in Sal's mind, he did not recognize his son and thought a stranger had entered his domain and needed to be removed, immediately. Matthew started to defend himself, which only lead to an angrier exchange.

To calm down the situation, I suggested Matthew exit out the front door, wait a few minutes, then return using the back door. "Come back in, say 'hi Pops', as if you just arrived. That is what I do when he gets like this. It usually works."

This was advice I had acquired through trial and error. Sal would see me as a threat, an unknown person, thief, or murderer, who knows? I learned to leave the house, so his perceived danger was no longer there, then return in another door, as his wife, happy to be home from work, or wherever. Usually, this trick worked like a charm.

With this suggestion Matthew did just that. When he came back inside, with a big "Hey Pops!" and a bear hug, Sal smiled and told Matthew he was glad to see him. Advice taken; lesson learned.

I always enjoyed Matthew's persona: generally easy going, friendly, caring, and almost always ready with a big smile, a hug, a sharing that life was good, and an unmistakable laugh that could make you want to join in whatever had caught his funny bone. It was his nature. Matthew had always been easy to get along with. Rare were the episodes where he could be difficult, after all, he was no perfect angel. Over the years he had minor brushes with the law, dumb mistakes, nothing major. He might drink a bit too much now and then, a period or two of melancholy, but mostly he was a gentle soul. He was a favorite son, a friend, a nice person to hang out with.

After several days of helping, running errands, and getting started on our new business venture, Matthew decided he needed to head back to Phoenix. Knowing the business would be months before start up, he decided that it was time to look for a part- time job to make ends meet.

Matthew was also looking forward to the regular Sunday hike, a routine he had missed the previous two weekends. He had joined an atheist hikers club, meeting every weekend for a nice Arizona hike followed by a visit to a local brew pub. Who could ask for more, a beautiful day in nature and a beer, with like-minded friends and engaging conversations, no doubt. I was a bit surprised he was hanging out with a group of atheists and wanted to know more. My question "why atheists?" turned into a philosophical discussion about religion, God, life and death, and a deeper, more meaningful prophetic conversation ensued.

I remember we were standing in the kitchen, enjoying a quiet afternoon. Sal was settled in the living room, dozing off and on in front of the television. For a little while, uninterrupted, my son and I shared an unforgettable exchange of ideas, opinions, and views. Looking back, in many ways, I recognized we shared a bit of our hearts and souls that afternoon. In fact, we were in the process of opening up to areas we had never discussed before.

I recall explaining my perspective regarding how our souls have some input into a wide range of possibilities in our upcoming life, before we are even born. I expressed to Matthew my belief that we are allowed a choice in our life to come: our family situation, our parents, and some of the conditions we will be dealing with as humans during the course of our time here.

I could not define when, or how, I had developed this idea, but I told Matthew that I was very happy he had chosen Sal and I to be his parents. He looked at me a bit puzzled, but seemed to accept that it was possible, though maybe a bit unbelievable.

We talked for most of that afternoon, and would have carried on a bit longer, but the day was getting late, and Matthew was eager to get going.

I told Matthew that I loved him more than anyone else in this world. After giving one another huge bear hugs, soon Matthew kissed his Pops goodbye. Next, he drove away in his truck. His dog Abby was sitting next to him. She always did that.

I was so proud of him. Yes, and so very glad Matthew had picked us to be his family. He really was a gift from the universe, in more ways than I could imagine.

Little did I know, as I waved goodbye, that days later, Matthew would face the ultimate ordeal, the test of his life in an event that would forever change my life.

A Morning in the Life
of a Caregiver

Three days after Matthew headed down the road with Abby for his planned adventures, I rose from my bed to greet an extra cold and cloudless January morning. This was long before the sun could dare to wake the neighbor's rooster.

It had been a rough night—one of too many nights spent like this. Sal had one of those restless and difficult sleepless episodes. My abilities as a caretaker were strained; it was simply impossible to get any sleep. A good night's rest was elusive, at best.

I had been startled awake early that dark morning to Sal crying out in eagerness, "Mama! Mama!" I didn't think much of it. Not at this point, anyway. True enough, he had been calling out for her often during many of the preceding nights. *Why* was a question I could not answer. Somewhere, in the fogginess of his mind, he was searching for maternal comfort. I pretended to assume her persona, and softly in a fond whisper: *"que quieres mijo?* What do you need, son?"

Sal responded that he needed his pants, and that he was going to be late for work. In Spanish, I replied that it was not a workday, no need to get up, just go back to sleep. He listened, still a bit confused, but settled down. After aiding him with a trip to the bathroom, I got him back to bed. Somewhat calmed down, he closed his eyes, and soon slipped back into a fitful sleep. I too dived under the covers, put aside my worries for a little while, and fell back into the land of dreams, a place where one could drift off without interruptions.

A little later, I heard a loud noise. I rolled over and saw Sal in quite a desperate predicament. He had slid partially out of bed. He was stuck. Somehow, he had managed to get entangled with the grab bar at the side of the bed. He was also buck naked, having removed his night clothing, for some unknown reason. The sight was a little bit funny, yet very disturbing at the same time.

I suppressed a sly smile and tried to rescue him. After some struggle with the weight of his heavy frame, I was able to extricate him from the bars, get him back onto his feet, and finally, get him back into bed. As I helped get his clothes back on, I asked where he thought he was going.

"To work" was his stark reply. This was a typical night: my trying to sleep, and his trying to deal with what the ultimate reality of his dreams looked like: there was nothing like the inborn ability of imagining he needed to get up and go to work, a life of taking care of his family responsibilities ingrained in his psyche.

Being a caregiver to your spouse is not an easy venture. Doubtless, I had choices. One decision might involve just giving up, walking away, and finding a new direction. Another possibility might involve my placing Sal in a care home. In that way, someone else could deal with his dementia. Was that a stress-free solution? How would I feel about myself if I did that? It was an untenable choice. It had nothing to do with time and space, nor money or freedom. It had to do with who I was and who Sal really was before his illness. He was my life, and I was his: "till death do us part" as the saying goes.

Meanwhile, I could choose to stay present at home and care for a man who was slipping away, which during that fateful morning included becoming helplessly trapped in between the grab bars and getting caught between several worlds. The decision to care for Sal felt like the most difficult path, but it also appeared as the most obvious choice to make.

Nevertheless, it was a choice that represented only a small measure of the love and compassion I felt for this man. He had been my husband for 35 years. Patience might be strained; it would not be easy going forward. How could I do what I had to do and do it well? It would be impossible to foretell at this critical point how the future would unfold.

Pondering my situation and compounded by worry, I fell into a dark hole, not the first time, nor the last. Most mornings I travelled down that road of self-pity. Often over the course of recent weeks, I had faced tragic moments with this man who was not always there mentally. I wondered if his true soul knew what his physical mind was doing. Surely this man whom I loved would never want to hurt me—and yet, time and time again, there it was. Angry words, accusations, not seeing me but reacting to the drama in his head—I faced incidents of his imagination almost daily.

I had moments where the thought of ending this relationship bounced around in my head. Should I run away? What if I put him in a home? What if he gets violent? I was at a loss on what to expect as he got worse, knowing that the day would come when he would move on, leave this world, this body, and go to a better place. Could I be there until he goes, help him through that commitment, that 'til death do us part covenant made years ago?

I mourned the life we had led, was depressed about the life we were living, and feared the life, and loss, that was coming. In my mind, I asked God: *WHY? Why Sal, why Lewy, why me, and why now?* I waited for a response. No answer came.

Occasionally a morning of reflection, tears, and a little time for self-pity were important and necessary for me to re-group, compose myself, and get ready for whatever was coming. I gathered up my thoughts, my willpower, and prepared for another day. Who knew what surprises were in store as time marched on in this exceedingly difficult journey.

Heavenly Vision

Matthew called later that morning, and I shared with him the unusual circumstance in which I had found Sal earlier that day, tangled up in the bed rail, in his birthday suit. To tell the truth, we even indulged in sharing a little laugh together. To be able to hang onto a crazy bit of humor in the light of Sal's predicament seemed a wonderful gift.

Matthew was in a great mood; excitedly he shared with me an experience after he had left my house two days earlier. That evening, he spent the night with friends in the area. It was one of those evenings when he wanted to hang out with his buddies, have a few beers and laugh and argue which football team was going to win the upcoming Super Bowl. He woke before sunrise the next morning and headed off to join his hiker's group for the planned Sunday morning trek.

The highway from Prescott to Phoenix serves as a road

marked by winding curves. Throughout mountains and valleys, the scenery changes from high desert scrub with plenty of junipers and grassland to desert saguaros, palo verde trees and ocotillo branches shooting up from the ground.

Enthusiastically, Matthew shared his wonderment on that Sunday morning drive. "Mom, it was so incredibly beautiful! I woke up super early; it was still dark when I left C.J.'s house. Stars were still shining. A few miles down the road, I ran into some heavy fog. Soon, as the sun began coming up, the moment it began shining over the mountain peaks, bright rays lit up all the mist."

Matthew continued with his saga, an experience filled with beauty and joy.

"What I saw next was incredible! There were dozens of little rainbows spreading out in front of me everywhere. It was magic, sheer magic! It seemed as if I were driving in a dream. I was thinking, 'Mom, do you think that is what heaven might look like?' Maybe, that is what heaven really does look like. It was the most beautiful morning I can ever recall seeing. I know you would have loved it, all of it. I wish you had been there to see the whole thing!"

I was struck by the tone of his voice. He had a deeply emotional response to what had been a singular experience of absorbing and soaking in all the beauty of that marvelous morning. Matthew was not one who would often reveal his innermost feelings in order to expand upon his singular enjoyment of spectacular events or experiences. All this was then a big surprise. I could scarcely believe that he was being this effusive and so open.

That memory he shared about the nature of his vision filled with magical rainbow mists seemed to have touched his soul to its deepest core. Matthew sounded so very excited about what had happened, and I was happy for him, too. There was no way I could not be overwhelmed with feelings of gratitude and joy at what he had described.

Changing the subject to something more down to earth, Matthew later relayed that he had found a good chance at getting a part- time job. In fact, he asked me for input as he was completing the last lines of the job application form.

"The brew pub wants to hire me as a part-time Brewmeister. That seems really kind of cool. While being in that position, I can learn how to make excellent beer. What should I put down as my qualifications?" Matthew really wanted the job. I could sense it. Nothing could possibly stop him now.

I responded with "Well, you could say, 'I am super-qualified because I love to drink beer.'"

"Ha, ha, ha mom, very funny!" he chuckled.

We laughed. I do not recall any maternal advice kicking in that would detail exactly what he should write down on his application. I just figured that Matthew had banished any real worries about his ability to nail the job down. The manager knew Matthew, so, obviously, the job was his and was around the corner waiting for him. In short, filling out the application was a mere formality.

Matthew finished his call; he said he planned to attend a seminar related to working towards his contractor's license later that evening. He promised to head up to see us the next morning.

My brother was facing surgery for colon cancer later in the week; I was going to help him with whatever was necessary to get him to the hospital as well as any other added support he might require. I needed Matthew to stay and take care of Sal while I could go and help my brother out. Life was a bit challenging that week, with two family members needing care. It was a blessing that Matthew was available to help.

That phone call from Matthew helped to put me in a great mood. We ended with the usual "I love you!" and "I love you, too!" closing, and I hung up. For a little while, my world seemed okay. Grateful for raising a dutiful, loyal, and good son, I thanked God for the gift of this boy of mine, my only son.

COSMIC INTERLUDE

Sal was in a decent mood throughout the rest of that wintry day. I shared my phone conversation with Matthew, and Sal smiled and commented that it was a nice story about the fog and the misty rainbows. Later in the day, after the evening meal, we settled into the living room and turned on the television.

The President of the U.S. was giving his annual State of the Union speech. As retired civil servants, my husband and I had long held an ever-deepening interest in politics. It had been our habit to watch the annual State of the Union speech and share a thoughtful discussion in its wake and at its conclusion.

However, this year was different. Because of his Lewy Body Dementia, Sal could no longer focus on anything for any length of time, let alone a long political speech.

I struggled to steel myself for an emotionally tiring and

arduous task. Most evenings, since dementia had gotten Sal in its grip, he would become restless and agitated; finally, he would begin to hallucinate. This was the routine almost every evening. There was no respite. I was alone in knowing how I would deal with the situation every evening.

Hoping that we could listen to the discourse, without Sal getting distracted, upset, or restless, I settled with him on the sofa and tried to focus his attention on what was happening on the television screen.

Imagine my surprise when Sal acted perfectly serene that evening, very unusual. We watched television in total peace. Glad that Sal was quiet, for a change, I placed my focus on the activity going on with the program and settled in for the speech. Although I felt immense gratitude for this radically different and tranquil evening, I could not help but wonder: *Why is Sal's dementia being kept at bay tonight? Is this night any different from any other? Can I believe that the stars are still twinkling in the sky? What is really going on? What lay beyond the curtain?*

Unexpectedly, my awareness shifted from staring at the television screen to a breath-taking light anomaly. Something inexplicable was happening, right before my eyes! Tiny colorful flashing lights magically appeared, twinkling inches away from my face. In fact, they were so close, I could almost reach out my hand and touch them.

Countless numbers of tiny specks danced in the air, resembling a sparkler, so popular from my childhood during Fourth of July celebrations. Bright pinpoints of color, clearer than anything I had ever seen!

These delicate lights glimmered for several seconds, holding my utmost attention, and then suddenly disappeared. *"What on Earth was that?"* I wondered as I glanced over at Sal, hoping he may have seen this fantastic display. On his part, he was still intently scrutinizing the television screen.

That made the situation more mysterious. Sal was totally unaware as to what I had just seen. I began to wonder if I was the only one who saw this unusual phenomenon. Was I hallucinating? That would not be good if my mind was beginning to see things too. The thought of both Sal and I wandering around the house, lost in our fantasies, was a bit disconcerting.

Before I could utter a word to Sal about what I'd seen, the sparkling lights appeared again! This time they were shining even more brightly than before. The lights were shimmering and hovering in front of Sal, in his line of vision as he was staring at the television. Attention seeking little stars, trying to communicate an important message to him? "Surely he sees them, not two feet from his face!" I thought to myself. "Why is he not reacting?"

Sal looked straight ahead, focused on the television broadcast, oblivious to the miracle playing out in front of him. Before I could blurt "look at that" or "what in the world" or "are you seeing what I'm seeing?" the sparkly apparition faded away. I could not understand what was happening, right in front of us, how it was that Sal was not reacting. The thought crossed my mind that maybe he did see them. I pondered that maybe this was just a normal occurrence in his world of dementia. I just had no answers.

Of course, now I began to wonder about my sanity. Am I hallucinating? Like Sal, am I having imaginary visions? Is dementia contagious?

No sooner did that worry cross my mind, than the lights appeared once again, flickering and shouting out for my attention. Hovering mid-air for a few moments, they drifted to my left, stopping for a short time just a few spare inches above a side table. A repeat performance of pinpoints, colors, sparkles so mesmerizing I almost forgot where I was. I sat and stared and reached out to touch them. That move seemed to scare them away. As quickly as they had lit up my life, they melted away into the darkness. For a moment I just sat, transfixed on the spot where they had disappeared, finally deciding that "Yes, I am losing my mind! God help us."

Watching that dark spot, wondering if the magic would come again, I glanced down. There on the little side table was a book, one that I had not recalled sitting there earlier that day. Like a dog who just saw a squirrel, my interest quickly shifted from one unusual happenstance to another. I noted the title of the book that oddly was placed on that table, and my heart began racing, pounding, dancing with glee! What was going on? I recognized the importance of this book in my path of understanding life and the formation of my spiritual development.

This book was *The Story of Edgar Cayce There Is a River*, by author Thomas Sugrue. Excitedly, I remembered, *"Oh, that's the book! That is what I read so many years ago; that's the book that influenced my belief that children consciously choose their parents. I told Matthew about this, just the other day when we were talking."*

I picked up the book, opened it and went straight to the pages of the section I had read decades before. Right to the place where Edgar Cayce explains the concept that I had presented in my discussion with Matthew. The idea that before we are born, our souls are given some clear choices on upcoming physical incarnations. Such choices include reviewing potential parents and family dynamics and having some say as to which life path would serve our greater goals.

"This is great! When Matthew comes tomorrow, I will be sure to show him this passage in the book."

Distracted by the book, I ignored the President's speech on the television. Instead, I recalled my conversation with Matthew before he headed to Phoenix, three days earlier. At the time, I told Matthew that I believed that, before our physical birthing, our young souls sit up in heaven waiting until they are given certain options as to what kind of parents they will need to choose. Later, we plummet down to earth and start working on our life mission, full of hope, ready for whatever the path would lead. It just seemed important to have shared this with him, at the time. Maybe he was finally ready to listen to my philosophy on life, no matter how crazy it could sound. It was time.

Matthew had promised to show up the next morning to help me care for Sal. I could not wait to tell him about the fascinating spectacle of lights and share with him the section from Edgar Cayce's book. Ignoring the President's speech, I continued to read, much more interested in the storyline than in listening to dry political speech.

How strange it was that Sal continued to quietly watch the television screen, as calm as a kitten. Even more interesting is that Sal would comment on parts of the speech, reacting to the presentation like he would in the days before dementia. I set the book down and interacted in a brief political discussion with Sal—a rare treasure, if only for a little while. He even went to bed afterwards with absolutely no hesitation.

It was nice to have Sal for one brief evening as if untouched by his dementia. I yearned for more, a return to the man he used to be. Maybe I could ask for a little miracle, inspired by the possibility that if stars can twinkle in my life— right in front of me, in my own living room—it wouldn't be far-fetched to make a wish. Wouldn't it be wonderful if those little stars were sent to heal my husband, pull out that awful dementia, and get him back to normal? Oh, if only that could be true. Hope sprung eternal, at least for one night.

Why Do Bluebirds Fly?

The next morning, I woke up to the beginning of another bright, sunny, and cold wintry day. Sal had slept unusually well, a rare and welcome pleasure. It would be such a blessing if this could be the daily norm. Thoughts of the incredible apparition of lights from the night before, the discovery of the Cayce book sitting out for my review, and Sal acting like his old self, for a little while, had me excited yet wondering why so much magic in just one evening. I could not wait to share my experiences with Matthew later that day.

I dressed and prepared for another day. Stepping outside, I braced for a breath of cold fresh air, a jolt to truly wake me up that early in the day. The rising sun warmed my face. I filled my lungs and felt refreshed, especially because I had just risen from the first peaceful night of sleep in a very long time.

Life had tossed challenges my way, yet, on that day, it

seemed a dark cloud or two had lifted. Would this serve as a reassuring presence? Would Sal sleep through the entire night on at least one more occasion? I knew nothing of the future, but hope was abundant.

As was my daily routine, I drove down the rural, dirt road in front of our home in order to retrieve the daily newspaper. The repository for the periodical was by the highway, almost a mile from the house. Too far to walk on a cold day, but a nice short drive past the scattered homes and horses, fields of dry grass and brush, on a bumpy washboard road.

Suddenly, I noticed something unusual, a large flock of bluebirds, a very rare sighting in our area. They were sweeping across a field, towards me, enjoying a morning flight. Swooping closer, they shifted their direction and began to fly alongside the car. This collection of bluebirds went with me on every inch of the drive, brilliant splashes of bright blue feathers weaving back and forth in unison with my vehicle.

Surprised, I felt blessed by their presence. Seeing them triggered a memory of my son Matthew as a young child. I could see him as a little kid, singing a chorus of the "Zip-A-Dee-Doo-Dah" song, emphasizing the part with "Mister Bluebird on my shoulder."

That long ago memory of my little boy singing filled my heart. As I watched the flock that moved so perfectly in unison, I envied the carefree motions, crisscrossing and gliding across the road straight in front of me. A nice reminder of happier times. That's all I thought about. That's all I could think about. What else had the day in store for me?

Returning home after retrieving the paper, I was filled with many pleasant thoughts. Bluebirds in the morning, sparklers the night before, so much magic and mystery. Peaceful, uninterrupted sleep and an evening discussion with Sal, just like the times long ago, before his world began to take him away.

All in all, the day seemed a little brighter. Lately, life had become increasingly challenging. Taking care of Sal, up to that point, had been the toughest experience for me to manage. That morning, however, my worries seemed to diminish and melted into the background, at least for a little while. A new day was dawning.

Upon my return from the short trip to pick up the morning newspaper, I set about getting breakfast ready. I helped my husband to get out of bed, got him dressed, and steered him towards the dining table. Sal appeared to be in a good mood, hungry, yet unusually calm and quiet. So far so good! It certainly began to feel like change was in the air.

I was looking forward to Matthew's arrival later that day. I had already begun to organize the business aspect for the upcoming venture we had planned together. We needed time to discuss setting up a name for our approaching enterprise, file the name with the proper government agencies, set up an account and insurance, as well as a variety of other tasks related to getting the license granted. Of course, these plans were made on the assumption that all the exams would go smoothly without a glitch.

I recall chattering away to Sal as we were enjoying

breakfast. "Matthew is coming up today. We are getting ready to put his contracting business together. He and I are preparing for the exam and setting up everything like a business name and whatever else needs to happen. I am glad that he has finally decided to move forward with this. Besides, it gives me something to do." Sal's big response was "That's nice. It's about time he got serious with life. And it gives you something to do."

Unfortunately, his awareness began to wane, and Sal started to lose interest in finishing his breakfast. He pushed at the table, and trying to stand up, he nearly fell and grabbed my nearby arm in desperation. Unsteady and eager to head to the living room, he started to get upset. *Oh wow!* Sal's ever-present adversary Lewy was returning! Darn it.

I steadied Sal, walked him to the living room, and he settled into his recliner for a day of watching a nature themed show on television. I had learned not to let him watch anything that would be hard to follow. Any program that displayed violence or any other disturbing elements could seep into his thoughts and cause issues later, at times replaying a scene from a program that he thought was real and part of his experience.

On one occasion, Sal became very upset and accused me of surreptitiously hiding money under the floorboards. It took me some time to first calm him down, and more importantly, to figure out that he had watched a movie the night before that showcased a scene in which money had been hidden under floorboards. You can imagine that my choice of programming became very crucial after that incident.

Just as I got Sal settled into his routine, the phone rang.

I picked it up and noticed the caller ID: "Phoenix caller." I did not recognize the associated number on the display. My first thought was it could be a scam call, one of those all too common and irritating ones that I often ignore. You know those potentially fraudulent callers that carry on something like: "Hi, you have just won a vacation!" or "You have an outstanding debt that needs to be settled by noon today!" or "You have an arrest warrant that needs to be cleared now!" So irritating.

Then I remembered that Matthew had recently called from a friend's phone; he told me that had lost his cell phone for a day or so. Perhaps, he was calling to give me an update on when to expect him. His original plan was to get to the house early, suggesting I could have some time to meet up with a friend for lunch, or shopping, while he watched Sal. Though with Matthew, he rarely followed through on his original plans. No doubt, he had lost his phone again, and was calling to say he would be home later than planned. Knowing that is the usual case, I had not made plans to meet any of my old friends for lunch.

As I held onto the phone, I was still deciding whether to answer it and looked again at the caller ID. A little warning flag popped up in my mind. Yes, something was not right. Something felt different; as it turned out, my instinct was totally correct. Looking back at that moment, an irritating scammer would have been much more preferred than the person I heard from on the other end of the call.

WHEN CROSSING THE ROAD, BE SURE TO......

Holding the phone as it rang one more time, hoping it could be Matthew, I could not shake the feeling that something was not right. Call it intuition, those moments when your heart knows, and seconds later, your head understands. With a curious tone in my voice, and a cautious hello, I answered the phone.

I heard a man's voice in response; a voice I did not recognize. "Hello ma'am, this is Detective Leo with the Phoenix Police Department."

My breath held, frozen. This could not be good. Experience reminded me that police only call if something is terribly wrong. They are the bearers of bad news.

"Do you know a Matthew Helmick?" he asked.

Oh no! my thoughts were racing uncontrollably. Is my Matthew in trouble? What did he do? Did he get arrested? Is he in jail, or worse, is he in the hospital? My heart started pounding; the pressure was too great as it came shooting up into my skull. This was not a question I wanted to hear, especially not in a phone call from a police detective.

I exhaled with what seemed the last bit of breath that could possibly maintain the shell of my outer sanity and cool. Thoughts of earlier times when Matthew had some troubles flooded through my mind. More than once, he had been picked up, calling from the jail that he was in a bit of trouble, could we come help. Nothing too serious, just his luck to be a magnet for traffic enforcement—but never before had a detective called.

Shaking now, I responded: "Yes, I am his mother."

Words can be so powerful, that, when spoken aloud, human souls can become crushed, broken, wounded, and forever changed. The next words that came through that phone in my hand were the most forbidden words imaginable. Jumbled and flowing and not making sense, yet there it was.

It does not matter one's race, culture or religion, economic status or level of education, or any other attribute that separates humanity into any class position or role in society. The words I heard are the words that no mother, no father, nor any parental figure would ever want to hear. Never!

"I am sorry to inform you, but your son has died."

A whirlwind of emotions, thoughts, fears, and anger swirled through me. An invisible force seemed to knock me off my feet. I threw myself into a nearby chair and collapsed in total disbelief. My heart pounded, blood rushed into my head and everything that had ever existed in my body throbbed and shook as if I had become shell-shocked in a violent earthquake of disbelief, despair, and incredulous defeat. How could this happen? This can't be true. He is lying. Why do people lie to me? Every day, they just lie.

Whatever I was going through, more words kept coming, flooding my senses. They have never stopped.

Now the voice on the phone said, "Matthew was killed last night in a hit and run accident."

And there it was. The end of my world as a mother to this, my only son whom I loved so dearly and so completely and with my whole heart wrapped around him.

From that first moment, when I first heard and knew that a baby had ever been on the way, I loved him. Matthew was the child I carried despite a rough pregnancy and multiple complications, the newborn baby who looked so angelic. I chose the name Matthew, which means "God's gift", for that is what he was to me. This was the boy who cried and laughed and played and grew into a gentle and vibrant young man. He had so much potential and so much energy. He had so many ideas and so many goals. He was a living, breathing human being with a heart. Now he was gone.

How could this be? No one and nothing could ever take him away from me. Not in this way! Maybe this was a crank call, a cruel joke, after all. I still could not believe Fate would choose him. Why me, why him, why now? This was Cayce's book unfolding with a new plot twist. How could our destinies choose such a conclusion to an otherwise loving and beautiful life? How could I ever be grateful again? How could I live?

So much love, so many emotional stories as well as so many fears zipped and sliced through me in nanoseconds of time that it felt like a forever pain. A whole life, Matthew's entire life story from beginning to end, was now frozen in outer space, somewhere where I could not go, and he could not visit. That is what I thought. If his life had ended, mine had also. Yet there I was alive and breathing and acting as if I always had control over my life in front of me.

"No, no, NO!" I cried. How is this possible? What happened? I needed to know the where and the when. Do you think a detective could manage this outcry? I cried to know every detail of how he had passed.

Despite my emotions almost compelling me to take immediate action, wanting to throw the phone down and put an end to all this nightmarish news, I wanted all the answers. I demanded the answers, not this week, but right now, I could not wait. *If you are going to kill me, do it now. Now!* How could I be sure this was not a dream or a hellish, fiendish trick someone was playing on me?

The detective knew his job. He obliged me.

"The initial investigation shows that last night Mr. Helmick was crossing 23rd Avenue at the intersection with Maryland. A car traveling north, speeding up 23rd, hit him and did not stop. He probably died on impact. We found his wallet with his address, went to the house but no one was there. I came back this morning to question the neighbors and find out if anyone knew his family. Someone gave me your name and number; sorry, we did not contact you sooner. Did he have a dog?"

Holding down my emotions, I needed to gather my wits and respond, "Yes, is she, is the dog doing all right?"

The detective replied that when he went over to the neighborhood, this very same morning, there was a dog at Matthew's address. Meanwhile, she would not let anyone get near or approach her or touch her. I thanked the detective for leaving the dog alone and said I would have someone come and get her.

In my mind, I was grateful that Matthew's dog, Abby, was okay, and worried that she had been alone and probably frightened all night. If Matthew was hit on 23rd Avenue, he had probably been crossing the street to take Abby to the dog park, a nightly ritual.

Poor Abby must have been with him when it happened, whatever it was that happened. A witness to her human's demise. No doubt, she was heartbroken and very scared.

I asked for more information. Specifics as to what had happened. I needed details that could fill all the slack in my imagination.

Detective Leo did share a little more, the facts of the investigation that were known, for the moment. "The accident occurred at about 7 pm. A call came into 911 just after 7 and the responders were there within five minutes. It looks like he was walking east across 23rd Avenue heading towards the park. The car seemed to hit Mr. Helmick just before he reached the other side of the street, the sidewalk. Specifically, he was in the bike lane when he got hit."

He continued. "The driver took off but then called back an hour later and turned himself in. The young man said he did not realize he had hit someone. Initially, he thought maybe he had hit a bicycle, but did not recall seeing a person. Thought there may have been a dog nearby but was not sure. He got scared, and that's why he kept going.

Our investigation will try to determine the driver's condition, impairment, or other factors that could have caused this accident. I can keep you informed. By the way, I have your son's wallet, but his keys are at the medical examiner's office. It will be days before I can retrieve them and arrange to get them back to you."

The detective offered me a little more information, but my head was crammed full of words spinning all about; what the words were communicating, and what the words meant and what words sounded like were mostly the ones that made little or no sense at all. You tell me if I could have absorbed any more details or specific data without losing it entirely! What do you think? Truly, there was little more data I could successfully absorb at this point. The detective closed by saying he was sorry and would keep me informed as to any new updates.

I hung up. My world was shattered. The unimaginable, horrible forbidden, and unthinkable words had all been spoken. My heart broke into a million pieces. I wanted to scream and cry and throw that phone across the room. I wanted to allow myself to dissolve into a puddle of tears.

Thoughts echoed, ricocheted, and then they actually felt as if they were banging against my brain. How could this be? What is happening? Why now? Why did this happen to my Matthew?

How is such an accident even possible? Nothing made any sense. Why was he walking in the street, as a car was fast approaching? Why didn't he look both ways before crossing that street? He had been taught from an early age to never cross a road without looking both ways. When taking the dogs for a walk, he had always been so careful, teaching them to also stop and look before going ahead. What do I do now? What the hell? My world fell apart. The weight of the mountain of hope for my son came crashing down, burying me in its wake.

There I was, deep in the middle of a mess, full-time caregiver to a man who was slipping away every day, bit by bit. Here, living in our home that Sal, Matthew, and I had built from the ground up.

There was no one with me at that moment that I could turn to comfort me or join me in my grief. My relatives, siblings, and Sal's children were all older adults who lived far away—none of the relatives in a position to be of any immediate help. There was no one to run to. No one to hold me up or support me. At that moment in my deepest state of grief, the loss of my only child was too overwhelming to contemplate.

I knew Sal was beyond understanding exactly what had happened. I had to do this journey all by myself. I was alone. Totally alone. All by myself.

I gathered my tears, thoughts, composure, and approached Sal, who had been deeply immersed in watching a nature program. I knelt in front of him, tears on my cheeks, trying to find the best way to tell him the tragic news.

"Sal, I just got off the phone. A police officer called. He said Matthew was hit by a car last night, he was killed. Matthew is dead."

I sobbed and choked on the words. Sal looked at me and replied, "I'm sorry" and gave me a little hug and a pat on my head. Even that was a miracle. It was all he could do!

Sal did not show any emotion, nor did he say anything about Matthew. Did he even fully recognize the fact that Matthew, this kid he had raised from birth, was no longer walking this earth? He responded to me as if I had come to him with a small cut on my finger. He would be the one chosen to just paste a kiss on it and then go on living as if nothing had happened.

Sal felt like a small child who could not understand death and its finality. He was wrapped up in the grip of his own new world, detached from everything that happened outside his bubble. The bubble of my grief was much larger than his world. I was not alone. Yet I was alone. More alone than I had ever been before. A strange kind of aloneness. At that moment I just wanted to crawl up into a ball and die.

Heartbreak

Minutes before, after we had finished breakfast, when my world was only challenging but not crushing, moments before that phone rang, my thoughts were on the future. My vision of where life was going to be taking us was altered by one single moment in time. A whirlwind of emotions, grief, tears, consumed me. How was this possible, this tragedy, at this already challenging point in my life? And Matthew's life, just starting to settle into a future? The dream to see your children's children, spoiling the little ones rotten, all the joys of a storybook life that was well- lived—all that ended in one horrible moment.

There was no panic room I could enter to scream or lock myself out from the tragic reality of death. Nor was there an escape into hours, minutes, or weeks of heavy grief. I had little opportunity to collapse into a ball of pain, sink into the depths of loss, set aside life until a glimmer of hope could lead me out of the despair, weeks, years away.

Caring for my husband required all my focus, my energy. No kidding, which was the only way I could move forward. I had to push myself out of the rubble and begin living in a new sense of reality. What was my new world going to look like? The future was not clear to me, if at all.

Sal needed attention. Calls needed to be made. Plans for a funeral, and services, and I was not sure what else had to be organized. Though my head was spinning, I had to pull it together and move forward with the next steps. Life could not wait on my emotions. Not right now.

My first call was to Matthew's girlfriend, Alex. She answered the phone with her cheerful drawn-out "Hellooo" and "How are you? I haven't talked to you in a while because I have been so busy over here." Alex was always a pleasure to talk to, easy to accept as one of the family, and, though not yet married to my son, she felt like a daughter in law. How could I bear to share the bad news?

Matthew and Alex had met a few years before. They had dated, at times lived together, and were a well-matched couple. At this juncture in their relationship, they were on a little break, each needing some space to regroup and figure out where they were going—two independent and head-strong personalities with big plans, not always on the same page.

I inhaled, tried to compose my crumbling emotions, and finally said, "Hi Alex, I have some bad news. Are you able to talk now?"

She answered me with a hint of sadness, an unusual

tone in her usual cheerful voice. "Well, no, I mean, yes. I mean I can talk. Is it Sal? What happened to Sal?"

"No, Alex, it's Matthew." I started to choke on my words, tears came coursing down my cheeks, "He was hit by a car last night, near his house. I think he was taking Abby to the dog park because he was hit on 23rd Avenue, right on the bike path. I just got a call from the police telling me what happened. He's dead. Alex, Matthew is gone. I am so sorry."

Alex broke down, I could hear the shock overwhelm her voice, "No! No, this can't be! How could this ever happen? Not to Matt! No, not him!"

"I don't know, Alex; I just don't know. All I know is he was crossing the street to the park; a car came and hit him, and the car kept going. It happened last night. The police had trouble finding a family member to contact. They got my name and phone number this morning from one of the neighbors. I only got the call minutes ago."

Alex sobbed, "I can't believe this; I know he was always so careful crossing the street with the dogs, any of them. How could a car have hit him? The whole thing, well, to me, it just doesn't make any sense. Ana was supposed to have breakfast with Matt yesterday, but she overslept and missed going. I can't believe this."

Ana was Alex's daughter. At 20 years of age, she was very attached to Matthew. She called him her stepdad even though they had only been connected for a few years. Indeed, he served as her very own role model.

Through tears, Alex was composed enough to worry

about the dog. She asked, "And what about Abby? Is she okay? Was she with him?"

The thought of Abby feeling scared and maybe also in shock, was of a deep concern. Alex worked only minutes away from the house and I was over two hours away. I was in no shape to drop everything and run down to pick up Abby.

"Abby was not hit, but the police detective said she was on the porch at Matthew's house and seemed very scared. Is there any way you can go and get her? She needs a friend right now. I can't leave Sal alone and am in no shape to run all the way to Phoenix. Please, can you do that, or maybe call someone to help us right now?" I asked.

Alex responded "Yes, of course. I will leave right now and call you when I have her with me. I just can't believe this is all happening. Not Matt! I am so, very sorry. This is totally unreal."

I do not recall the rest of our conversation; I know it was not a long one. Fortunately, Alex was able to gather enough composure to excuse herself from her job, run over to Matthew's house, and pick up Abby. She called afterwards to let me know that both she and Abby were shaking and in shock. Offering to bring Abby to me, I asked Alex to wait, a little while, until we could calm down and manage any long drive down the highway. Neither of us were in the condition to handle traffic.

Next, I contacted my sisters. One lived in the midwest, the other on the east coast. They were as shocked as I. Matthew was their first nephew, and that bond was always a piece of their heart. They dropped everything going on in their lives at the time, booked the necessary flights, and arranged to spend the next several nights with me. I was not ready to tell my dad his first grandson was no longer with us. Thankfully, my sisters accepted that responsibility.

Calls to Sal's children were next. His daughter Patricia was devastated, and arranged to fly from Texas and help me for as long as was needed. Guillermo lived about 30 minutes away, and made himself available; he showed up soon after to help with his dad.

The next two hours I made the calls to my closest friends, Matthew's friends, anyone else for whom I kept a phone number, which had been a part of our lives in one way or another. Soon the house began to fill up with our mourning visitors, one after the other. The outpouring of love and support now flooded in from everywhere. Everything was unexpected. I was not alone, truly, for at least a little while.

My close friend, Buena, lived nearby. Shocked at the news, she dropped everything and drove over to lend her support. Buena was the biggest help those first few hours that horrid day. Her love and compassion held me up, and we made it through the next few hours. Later in the afternoon Alex called. We arranged to meet halfway, a mid-point, so she could deliver Abby.

Guillermo, arrived and was recruited to watch his dad, so I could leave for a little while to meet Alex. Buena offered to drive, knowing that my emotional state was not conducive to being behind the wheel. When we met up with Alex, poor

Abby was trembling and crying. She desperately wanted my complete attention. I hugged and held her tightly as Buena brought both of us back home.

Later that incredible and unbelievable dreadful day, I was alone once again. Buena and Guillermo were a godsend, as were the visitors who were able to stop by. All of the caring and outpouring of love helped me throughout those first hours of grief. By the evening, the visitors and helpers had departed.

I was alone with my thoughts. Sal had gone to bed early; Abby was anxious. She would lie on her bed a few minutes, then get up and go to the front door, waiting. I think she was expecting Matthew to pop in and give her a big hello. After a little wait she would walk over to me, get a hug, a pat on her head. Lay down again. And repeat.

As I sat alone that dark night, waiting for my sisters to arrive later that evening, I reviewed the events of the day. It had begun with a good night's sleep; Sal was calm and rather quiet at breakfast. There had been a beautiful sunrise and a magical drive, bluebirds at my side, a nice morning to lighten my mood.

The bluebirds were such a beautiful touch to the morning drive. I recalled the lyrics to the song, "Somewhere Over the Rainbow," and as the melody flooded into my saddened mind, I wondered to myself: "why, oh why can't I fly away like the bluebirds, and say this just never happened?"

My thoughts just rolled around, looking for answers. Why did a lovely day turn into the worst possible day ever?

Why were there bluebirds, and why did that song have them fly over a rainbow? What does that even mean? Were they a harbinger of the tragedy that was to unfold that morning? Were they signs, could they have been sent by Matthew? Was it a coincidence that those birds made me think of him, memories of childhood, on a morning following his death? Is that possible? So many questions rolled around in my tired, weary, exhausted mind. Nothing made sense to me, not anymore.

As my thoughts flowed, memories appeared. I recalled that December day a short few weeks ago when I was driving with Sal, in Phoenix. The day he had an outburst, a demand for me to immediately stop the car. Sal was adamant, "someone is going to get hit."

It struck me, suddenly, that the road we were travelling on when Sal insisted there was trouble ahead was the very same road Matthew was crossing when he got hit by a car and died. We were almost at that intersection where Matthew was hit that day Sal had his episode of fear.

This realization floored me. Had Sal sensed something that was bound to happen, but at a future point? A tragedy that played in his mind, a prelude of things to come? I could not wrap my head around the possibility that, unknowingly, Sal had somehow predicted this horrible event as we approached the very spot where death came and grabbed our son, Matthew. A mystery. Something else that demanded attention. My head hurt. Life had become a nightmare, and it was going from bad to worse.

NO TIME TO CRY

I had little time to collapse, to cry, to get lost in the emotions of this horrific tragedy. Plans had to be made. Do we have a funeral, or a cremation, or a celebration? The when, where, and how questions were hanging around needing a quick response. It was on my shoulders to find the answers. Thankfully, my family and close friends were there to help me.

We had two weeks to move through this new landscape and honor Matthew's life. With a few conversations, opinions, and phone calls I decided to do a cremation. My sisters and I met at the funeral home, joined by one of Matthew's closest buddies, and one of my oldest friends, to pay our respects before his body was cremated. We were told he suffered numerous broken bones; injuries so extensive that nothing more could be shown than his face. It was heartbreaking to see him, lifeless, wrapped from head to toe in a covering. Only his face, looking at peace, was showing evidence of the trauma visible on his forehead and chin. I could not imagine the pain he must have endured.

A celebration of life seemed much more appropriate. Matthew would have loved to see us all raise a few toasts to his memory, and not be sitting in a drab church pew crying at a formal, churchy funeral. I recalled a story Matthew had shared with me months earlier, about a funeral he attended. An older friend of his, one who had been his mentor in many ways, had passed away to cancer. With death approaching, this man asked Matthew to be with him in those last moments of life. Matthew was asked by the family to give a little eulogy. Apparently, in line with his relationship with this fellow, an army vet who was a bit rough around the edges, Matthew stood up in front of that crowd in the church and shared some colorful tales about his friend. Not quite in keeping with the minister's request to keep things to a more sacred level—no, my son had to delve into a bit more of the profane side of life. No doubt his friend was laughing away from his seat in heaven, chugging a beer and enjoying Matthew's presentation.

Arrangements were made to host two farewell gatherings, one in Prescott at his favorite brew pub, the other in Phoenix at a friend's restaurant. Matthew had connections in both areas over the years, so it just seemed like the best way to send him off. He would like that, I was certain.

With help from friends and family we pulled together a nice memorial: photos in a video presentation, a lovely handout with more photos, and some poems and song lyrics. A few keepsakes to hand out. A collaborative effort by so many who loved him.

There was more that we needed to deal with in those two weeks. Sal needed his usual care; he did seem to enjoy the different women in his life for those few days and was rather cheerful to get all the attention. My brother had his surgery for colon cancer during all of this. Fortunately, that went well, and my sisters were available to help him. He recovered quickly enough to attend one of the celebrations.

With the assistance of my sisters and stepchildren, along with some of Matthew's friends, we were able to handle a variety of necessary tasks. Everyone chipped in. I was so grateful for all the help, and through it all, I held up pretty well. I had no other choice.

A Park, a Tree,
a Memory

Three days after Matthew died, my sisters and I drove down
to his home in Phoenix and met with the detective. He handed
over Matthew's wallet, his car keys, and supplied a little more
information on the status of his investigation.

Initial investigation reports were that the driver was
not impaired, not distracted by his cell phone; indeed, the accident was unintentional. The driver was going 10 miles over
the speed limit, probably much too fast to respond and avoid
hitting a pedestrian in the road. The young man insisted that
it all happened so fast; he did not see anything until he heard
a loud thump, an impression he hit something. Meanwhile, he
didn't really know what it was he had hit. He panicked, got
scared, and kept going.

The detective said it would be some weeks before the

investigation would be completed, but he was certain that the driver would face charges. The county attorney's office would be overseeing the specifics. In addition, he told me how to obtain all the requisite reports as was going to be necessary. I thanked him for keeping me informed.

The details of that night seemed so surreal, that a driver was speeding and could not recall seeing someone in the road, someone who was crossing over right in front of him. It seemed as though the driver thought he had hit a ghost. Yet, this was a phantom that went bump in the night and left some serious damage in its wake. It just seemed so improbable that the driver could be so careless.

After the detective left, my sisters and I walked to the scene of the accident, just one house over from Matthew's home. Crossing the street at the exact place where Matthew had taken his last steps was a very emotional experience for me, as my thoughts drifted to consider how he felt during his very last moments.

What had my son seen? What had he not seen? Why did he remain unseen, as if that driver hit a ghost? He was my son that I had birthed and was made of flesh and bones. Why hadn't he seen the approaching car? I wondered whether his last moments were filled with pain and suffering or, at best, did he feel nothing? All these thoughts swirled about in my brain. The thoughts were coming fast and were relentless. How would I ever see the world as a place of comfort, peace, and calm ever again?

In the park there was a large tree that was situated not

far from the place where Matthew had been hit. At the base of the tree, someone had left a gift, a vase with a big yellow ribbon wrapped around it. There was also a note, pinned on the trunk of the tree, which read: "Matt - 34 years. I will miss my buddy. I'm only 13, but he liked me. He helped me so much. Goodbye to my big buddy. Love Matthew."

My sisters and I were brought to immediate tears by this touching tribute left by a young friend who bore the exact same name.

Moments later, a man walked up to us and interrupted our sad reflections.

"Hi, I'm Lynn. I live just across the street. I don't want to bother you, but I just noticed you had all gathered here. Did you know the person who recently died here?"

I turned to Lynn and explained who I was, "Yes", I told him, "It was my son, Matthew. He had lived just down that street, right behind that house over there."

I pointed towards the row of homes that lined the western side of the road. Everything felt unreal and surreal, in fact.

Lynn looked like a very kind and compassionate soul; tears welled up in his eyes, and he shared his connection to the place of the accident. Glancing to where I had pointed, he shared his house was on the corner, the one directly behind it was Matthew's home.

He continued, "I am so sorry. My son is also named Matthew. He is the one who wrote the note and left the flowers. My son and your son were good friends. My son is only 13, but your son took a real interest in him, just like a big brother would. Your Matthew would leave my boy money. He often hid it under a rock in his driveway. That way my boy could have some surprise bit of spending money. I want you to know my son used to play football here, right here in the park with your son. Your son took an interest in my boy's life. I always appreciated it, because, after all, I am a single parent. With the bad leg that I have, I cannot really run around or go outside and play ball. My Matthew is really hurting over losing his best buddy and his best friend. His life will never be the same, either."

Hearing this connection, two Matthews, one park, one fraternal connection, I choked up. I had no idea that my son had ever served as such a role model for this young neighbor. What an incredible tribute was being paid to my son!

I replied that this was a beautiful sharing that was taking place, a thank you for the memories, touched by the realization at how Matthew was an inspiration for another. I was filled with so much gratitude. I was quick to thank Mr. Lynn for all the kind words of condolence he expressed. He wanted to tell us more and began to give more details as to what had happened that tragic night, just days before.

"The night of this accident I was sitting in my house; suddenly, I heard a loud pop noise outside the window. I headed out the door and saw some people over at the park, running and yelling to call 911. I picked up my phone and dialed for help. Within minutes, the paramedics arrived and started doing their work. My son and I crossed the street to get a closer look. All we could see was a body, lying lifeless against this tree, on the ground. The paramedics were working on him. I had no idea who he was because it was dark, and I did not want my son to get too close. I thought there was a dog nearby, but it was too dark to recognize that it could have been your son's dog.

"The next morning, a police officer came to the house and asked me if I had seen anything of the accident. She told me the name of the victim. I was shocked to learn who it was. He was such a nice guy. I am so sorry for your loss. If there is anything I can do, let me know."

Though Mr. Lynn's sharing of what had happened was most welcome, still and all, it was extremely difficult and very hard to listen to. We thanked him for sharing his experience. We especially cherished his connection with Matthew. So, there were two Matthews forever to be loved. We did promise to keep in touch.

My sisters and I looked at each other, almost in disbelief. Together, we said goodbye to the old tree, the last resting place for Matthew. The spot where he took his last breath. There were scratch marks in the dirt at the base of the trunk. "Was that blood mixed in the dirt?" we asked each other. We wondered if Abby had come back, after everyone had left that night, and had smelled the ground, dug into the earth to uncover her human. Was she sniffing out his presence in that hallowed ground?

I have never returned to that park. The memory is still too hard to bear: the tragic scene, those final moments of my son's life played out in my imagination, a never-ending nightmare. The fate of what had happened to Matthew was still too fresh in my mind to ever want to revisit his final resting spot again and relive the horror.

To this day, I still wonder what Matthew's last thoughts were. Why had he been so blind to the oncoming threat to risk crossing that road when he did? Especially with Abby, an unlit corner, that dark night? A path only lit by the bright headlights of an approaching vehicle. What was he thinking? Abby knew how to cross that road to the other side without getting hit. That was such a bittersweet detail to consider.

A Proper Farewell

The first of two celebrations of Matthew's life were held in Prescott at his favorite brew pub/restaurant, a place that Matthew had frequented over the years and where he had made friends with the owners and staff. The restaurant offered us space, food, beer, and drinks at minimal cost. There were at least a hundred people who came to share stories as well as their support for their loss and mine.

I brought Sal to this gathering, and for a little while he enjoyed himself, surrounded by familiar faces of family and friends. After an hour or so, Sal began to drift off into his dream world, and found himself amid strangers. The unfamiliar circumstances wore him down quickly, and he became anxious and confused half-way through the toasting and sharing of intensely enthusiastic stories. With help, we were able to get him into the car and his daughter took him home early.

A dear friend of ours in Phoenix hosted a second celebration at her restaurant in Phoenix the next day. I had left Sal at home in the care of his son, afraid that a long day in Phoenix would be too upsetting for him. It was another huge congregation of Matthew's neighbors, co-workers, friends, and others who knew him, from all walks of life.

Some of those who gathered at the Phoenix celebration were part of Matthew's Sunday morning hiking group; after all, he was a self-proclaimed member of the Atheist Hikers Club. They gifted me a portfolio, several beautiful photos of Matthew, taken over the previous months, on several hikes. Many of the pictures included his dog, Abby—a touching gift that I am forever thankful for.

A few of his other buddies were bikers, adorned in chains hanging from their belts, skull- themed tee shirts, heads wrapped in bandannas. They were an interesting group with rough-edged humor and stories of times with my son. Matthew was not a biker, but he seamlessly got along with everyone.

A small group of middle-aged guys came up, introduced themselves as fellow craft beer lovers. They had enjoyed Matthew's company at a local brew pub over the recent months, and presented a collection of monies, donations by patrons of the bar, to help the family, something they wanted to give in his memory of the good times and discussions of life, politics, the nature of sports, and all the stories that had been shared over beers at a favorite bar.

Several of my old friends, those who knew Sal and I

before Matthew was born, were also there to lend support, hugs and tears, and memories of better days—good friends who had been a part of our life throughout the years.

Time and again, stories were shared indicating the details of how Matthew had always helped others; there was no stranger who asked for help that he had ever turned down. Tales of his great sense of humor and a deep, infectious belly laugh circulated. Truly, he would be missed by all. Not a dry eye in the crowd!

It was tough to experience the loss of my son, but I was so glad that there was a family, a community. A busy two weeks of planning and preparing, reaching out to others, and receiving so much love and support, was ending. I was blessed to have so many people around me who cared. It had been the worst two weeks of my life, yet in ways, the most treasured time, surrounded by all that love and support.

In some ways, this brief, busy interlude of actions and celebrations kept me agreeably distracted from the depths of my own grief, at least for a time.

ROAD OF TEARS

Following that last celebration of life in Phoenix, after saying all my goodbyes, sharing hugs and tears, responding to so many offers of "If you need anything just call" moments, I climbed into my car and headed home. Now with a long two-hour drive lying ahead of me, I was alone, for a little while. The quiet solitude allowed my mind to wander.

For the first time in two weeks, I was totally by myself. The memory of Sal's last drive home from Phoenix, weeks earlier, served to warn me not to try another long road trip with him. His state of mind was not steady enough to rely on with any measure of support or safety. Instead, Sal remained at home, under the watchful eye of his son Guillermo. Doubtless, he must have wondered why the house was suddenly so quiet and empty in contrast to all those days of frenetic activity.

It felt a bit strange, yet I needed space to grieve, alone.

The recent days had been filled with so much love and support, yet not a lot of space to just sit quietly and feel my heart. To understand that a shift in my whole being was taking me to another place, to absorb that shock of a future without my son, had eluded me for a little while. Driving alone down the long familiar road allowed much needed time to think.

I could not replay the events of the past two weeks without feeling that I was a new person, one I had not yet had time to meet. Why didn't I know myself? What was the new me going to be like? How would I get by without knowing the details of what lay ahead? How could I trust the future would be bright? How could I trust myself not to be overwhelmed with feelings of loss and grief?

At this point, all my emotions punched in hard. Tears flowed, memories ran wild, and grief hit me with a sharpened, yet blunt edge of remorse, suffering, even thoughts of vengeance towards that driver that caused all of this chaos. Could I have protected my son from this accident? Could I have been a better parent? What did I do wrong? Did I miss something? Was there something I should have told him?

The road home was a long and well-known route as far as I was concerned. The drive was one that I had traveled often over the years. So many times, I swear I could go down that highway easily with both eyes tightly closed, like a robot in control of a driverless vehicle.

The familiar path held a few memories, moments over the years that involved travelling back and forth. There was the very place where once we had been detained due to an unforeseen accident. Matthew and I spotted a dog running loose along the road and had jumped out to rescue the dog from incurring an uncertain fate. Here is the place where Matthew nearly died when he drove home late one night, tired and fighting to stay awake, his truck clipped something, and he lost control. His truck had been badly damaged, but nonetheless, he survived a would-be fatal accident that time around. In fact, he made it through the whole frightening episode without a single scratch.

Another spot along the familiar highway called up the memory of a hot desert summer when we set about climbing the steep grade in an old Volkswagen bus. The bus died trying to chug up that road, and we were stranded for quite a while, in the blistering mid-day heat; we had to wait for a tow to the nearest garage, located many miles away. Thankfully, we had water, though it was not chilled. We survived.

A lot of memories over the years still pop up for me, whenever I find myself driving on that long stretch of road where so many events happened, and we emerged unscathed. I shifted into autopilot mode and allowed my mind to drift into a dangerous and deep emotional abyss. Two weeks prior, my son had been driving down this very same highway, but in the opposite direction. It was his very last trip down this overly and all too familiar route. This was a journey he would never make again. No, not ever!

Tears flowed, hard and fast; I could barely see. I cried continuously and kept on driving. I recalled the last time I hugged Matthew and the discussion we had held a few days before his passing. Suddenly, it struck me about the true nature of that conversation. In fact, it was the last time we were together and bonded as mother and son, locked in a deep and profound discussion.

Did we realize the full meaning of the discussion that afternoon, its relevance in light of what had just transpired? Do we ever completely realize what we are doing on Mother Earth?

We had discussed and summarized for each other the very nature of our lives. We shared the meaning of our birth, our purpose for being here; the hardship, suffering and other challenges in life. The essence of that exchange of ideas was, in review, an eerie premonition, a portent of what was to come. I had no clue what was coming. If Matthew knew, he never let on.

When Matthew left that afternoon, two weeks prior, neither of us realized that three days later he would no longer be walking this earth—and yet, maybe, just maybe, we did know something was coming. However, just what exactly, neither of us knew—something so big that would change our lives in ways we could not recognize or discern. Sal certainly felt something tragic was coming weeks before.

Looking back on that day, the conversation leading to areas we had never discussed before, it seemed as if a door to one chapter of life was beginning to close; words and emotions needed to be shared openly right at the perfect time. Evidently, another room, another door was leading us into a different world with fresh new eyes showing us an entirely altered perspective, eyes now focusing on a new landscape.

These thoughts, memories, and musings carried me home that evening. Delving deeper into our life pathways that had brought me to this crossroads, in that drive home alone, with no other distractions, allowed me to fully evaluate my last moments in the presence of my son, at the house, before he headed off on his adventure.

REFLECTIONS ON A LAST CONVERSATION

Days before Matthew crossed that tragic street, he was at our home, having just spent several days helping me with Sal. He had done a few chores around the house, tasks I had little time to focus on. Matthew also spent a little time running around town, picking up groceries and supplies, and running into old friends.

On that last afternoon, before heading out, Matthew told me had plans to go that evening to hang out with one of his pals, in Prescott, and then head down to Phoenix for a desert hike the next morning with a group he had joined, an atheist hikers club.

I asked him: "Why are you hanging out with atheists? I know you are not that religious, but why that particular group?" His reply mattered. "Mom, they are really nice people, and they never question anyone's beliefs. It's nice to hang around with people who don't judge you and allow you to be who you really are. That is my ideal situation!"

My son had always been open to a variety of perspectives, cultures, and belief systems. So, it all made sense to me that he would be comfortable around others who were apparently non-judgmental. I was a bit proud of this kid of mine who could embrace almost anyone without a narrow perspective, without prejudice.

Matthew's interest in atheists however, had sparked more conversation relating to religion and the basis for his thoughts on spiritual matters. We had not discussed deeply held beliefs for a long time. Once that magic door opened and we able to step aside, we began sharing our thoughts about religion, life and death, and exactly what we thought we were doing here on earth. One thing we both knew: how to be calm in the face of adversity.

At the time of our pivotal and magical conversation, I shared with Matthew my innermost thoughts. I told Matthew that though my upbringing was supposed to produce a good Catholic, someone very interested in going to church every Sunday and following all the proscribed rules and tenets of religion that later, at some pivotal stage in my life, I began to question.

If God was such a loving father, why would he punish each of us with specific challenges, especially if we were his beloved children who needed to be constantly reprimanded for all their little foibles and endless litany of mistakes in the confessional? Where was the line between forgiveness and responsibility, between compassion and cruelty? Between love and hate?

"Just look at Pops and the way in which he chose to punish you when you were little. Did he whip you or send you away or hurt you in any way? No! Because he loved you. He would talk to you, maybe just a bit more emphatically than normal, and encourage you to do better. True enough, he might tell you to go to your room and not ever beg to come out until you could behave in the right way. Meanwhile, you know it's true he never threatened you with bodily harm, nor an eternal kind of a hellfire ripe with damnation and flames. So, what kind of a father does religion create with a God who sends people to damnation for their mistakes? All this just does not make a bit of sense to me."

Matthew agreed. "Right, Mom! Why would religion create a God that is so mean? Shouldn't God be all about love? I would think that when I choose to die, my life would surely be weighed up as being worth something. I want to believe there is a heaven to go to. I don't want to be afraid of getting punished. I try to be a good person; so, why would God punish me because I don't go to church or because I don't believe in some religion when there are so many ideas on religion, anyway? That just does not feel right to me. I do not believe in hell. I think it is a made-up place used to scare people into obedience under false pretenses. The only hell we have is what happens here on earth sometimes. And that is it. That's all we must worry about."

I considered his points, and replied. "You know Matthew, there are some bad things that happen here. People who commit terrible acts and perform many horrible crimes. Life can really be hard, but I, too, feel that there is a better place for us once we leave this world. Maybe the bad people must atone for their actions once they leave here. Nevertheless, the thought of an eternal damnation or spending an eternity in hell just doesn't make any sense. No loving parent would want that for their children. So, why would God want anything like that for us? You tell me!"

The conversation sparked Matthew's easy and open sharing with me as to his own viewpoints and reflections on life. He said, "I have been learning about how everyone of us is living our own story, that my story is not yours, and yours is not mine." I asked him to clarify, as this was something I could not quite understand, even as a mother.

"Mom, you have your own way of looking at life, at me, at the world, as well as what you think and believe is true for you. You see the world from your viewpoint, but that is not the only or final truth. I have my own perspectives. You can't decide for me how my life should be lived. That is my choice. Besides, I am not even in a position to dictate to you or to tell you how to live your life. We each have to just live the way we think is right and not project our expectations on each other. That is really what I am trying to say so that I can clarify what I really believe."

I considered this response and could not quite understand exactly what he meant. However, no matter what, I still had a good feeling that Matthew was starting to delve into his own philosophy of life and had a keen sensibility as to what this place on Earth was and is all about.

I then shared more of my beliefs. At this point, I told Matthew that I believed he had a choice in this life. I felt he had a say in choosing his family, his parents, and maybe some of the circumstances for his life, even before he was born.

"Matthew, I have a belief that we live more than one life during our time on this planet. I also believe we come here many times to learn and grow and to try to act in the very best way we can be. Our lives are full of opportunities to face all kinds of challenges and hardships. We have to make decisions, to try and be better people. I think before we are born that we are given a choice to find out what we need for growing into the next life. Like, maybe, we are shown a map that has been previously shown to us. We will start at point A, our birth. Then we must make decisions in life; we can see the various pathways that can happen, depending on the choices we are afforded to make from the beginning of time. There is no good or bad; instead, there is just a multitude of situations to explore, to learn, and to grow. Eventually, we reach the end of that life. No matter which path we decide to take, the last moment here is inevitable. After that, we return to heaven, review that life, and then plan for another try at this thing called life. What a wild ride!"

Matthew looked at me with a puzzled face. "Are you saying that our whole life is planned, from birth to death? What about free will?" he asked.

I responded, "We are not stuck in a set plan; we are free to choose the directions, decisions, and the kind of lives we look to live. The only thing that seems certain is our birth and our death. The rest is up to us. When we are born; we are not meant to remember everything; otherwise, nothing would be interesting enough to attract our learning new and old aspects of our lives. I think that if we knew everything and we knew what was all lying ahead, there would be no room for growth. Most would take the easy way out and not the road that would teach us more and appear more challenging. I think we have a sense before birth of all the possibilities. But at birth we are plopped down, without that information on what is to come to guide us, and we move ahead down whichever road we choose along the way. Our decisions along the route all lead to the same destination; sometimes we have a rough time figuring that out."

Matthew looked at me, puzzled. "So, mom, my story is that when I was born, I had a life journey to follow, and I have made good decisions and some I regret, but, no matter what, I will be okay at the end of this. No right or wrong, no punishment after I die. That makes sense. Just one question, did I really choose to be your son before getting born?"

"I think you did, Matthew. Though maybe you were not always happy with that decision. We have had a few difficulties over the years. Still and all, I believe that before you took another chance at life on this planet, you looked over the possibilities and decided on us as your parents—which, by the way, I am so glad you did.

I really believe you chose me, and you chose Sal. I can't recall where this concept first popped into my head, but it is something I have believed for many years. Maybe we have done these lives together many times, I don't really know. I just hope this time around has worked out well for you, and us."

He pondered this idea, and replied, "Yes, that makes sense. You guys really have been great parents, and if that was my choice, right on!"

We discussed a little more about my ideas, and somehow got into a slightly different topic. "Matthew, I believe that when we die, we leave our human body, but we carry on forever as a soul, immortal. I am not sure about sitting around heaven with harps. Hopefully, our souls do something more enjoyable than that. That may be where reincarnation is a welcome opportunity to jump back in and experience the craziness of this planet.

"And I know that because life goes on, that when I do die—which will probably be long before you—that I will come back and give you a sign that I am still around. And I hope that should you go before I do, which would be most unusual, that you come and give me a sign. Agreed?"

He laughed a little, and smiled, and responded, "Sure, mom let's do that. Just don't go anytime soon because Pops needs you right now." We hugged, a good long hug. Matthew needed to get going, so we said goodbye, and he promised to be back in a few days.

Matthew walked over to Sal and said, "I love you Pops, I'll be back on Tuesday or Wednesday." He bent over and kissed Sal on the forehead. Sal smiled and grasped Matthew's hand, squeezed it, and said, "I love you too." Matthew called Abby to follow him, and they left the house, heading to the car for whatever adventure awaited.

This last conversation played in my head on that drive home following the Phoenix celebration for Matthew. Our discussion went into subjects that we rarely talked about: religion and philosophy of life, sharing our ideas about what this world is all about.

Looking back, I knew a door had opened, and our hearts merged. For a moment in time, we understood each other.

Days later, Matthew stepped through that door and closed it behind him, and I stayed here, wondering why. I wanted to follow him, to be done with this life and the challenges and sadness and despair heading my way. I wanted to go with Matthew to that other side, where God resides—but I could not. My other great love, my Sal, needed me. And I needed him, more than ever.

When I returned home from that long, lonely drive, my tears had run dry, and the chaos and sadness of the recent two weeks began to settle down. Going into the house, I needed a hug. Sal was sitting at the table, quietly focused on his dinner. I put my arms around him, and he pulled back, looked up, and asked "Who are you? When is Diane coming home?" I sighed, "Diane should be back any minute now." I had no tears left to cry for the man I was losing. My new normal was here, and I needed to brace myself for whatever was to come.

Having just survived the worst experience a mother could imagine, I was facing the immediate future with a spouse whose memories were lost. I knew it would be heartbreaking, but I was ready for the challenge. A new form of life was waiting for me, and I needed to keep moving forward.

At the beginning of the year Sal was slipping steadily into the grips of dementia, losing bits and pieces of his mind, his body, his essence. My role as caregiver for Sal was clear, but I had no idea how that would play out. Could I keep Sal home until it was his time to transition, or would we face placement in assisted living? Matthew was to be here to support me and help as best as he could, and I depended on him.

Now the world had changed.

The tragedy of losing Matthew was devastating on so many levels. Reflecting on those two weeks following his death, I knew the worst two weeks of my life were now behind me. What lay ahead was uncertainty and worry. My focus had to shift towards taking care of Sal, and the future looked grim.

I had just faced unexpected tragedy without falling apart. Grief had a chokehold on me, but I could still breathe. Whatever life was ready to throw my way, I could handle.

Sometimes miracles happen when you least expect them.

A PROMISE KEPT

In all this tragedy and death, dealing with loss and grief, preparing for the life ahead, I had been blessed with something that kept me going, a truly wonderful and phenomenal moment in time, one that was surreal, yet it made sense given the circumstances. This one brief glimpse into another world, which shifted my pain and grief just enough that I was able to make it through those first few days, weeks, months, and now years. It was a life changing miracle that continues to lead me into an altered state of reality today.

It was my son, Matthew, who reached out from death to show me a new path, one that carried my heart through the coming days, weeks, and now years.

The day that I received the call no parent ever wanted to hear had started with so much beauty and hope—a lovely, sunny day, bluebirds along my way—life was not so bad despite the road to come. I knew the coming months would be challenging with regards to my husband and his condition. I was prepared for what that would bring. However, I could never imagine being ready for that unexpected and tragic loss of my son.

After the detective had called with the bad news of Matthew's horrible passing. my day was filled with tears and reaching out to others. It was almost too much. By that evening, I was exhausted.

Sal had made it through the day without too much trouble and had gone to bed early. I stayed up late. My sisters were on their way to help hold me up and lend a hand. I was so grateful they were able to drop everything to come and support us.

In the days that followed, Matthew's dog Abby was with me and would not leave my side. Her eyes spoke of so much sadness, I wondered which one of us was having the hardest time processing the horror. I knew that the only reason Matthew would have been crossing the road towards the park was to take Abby for her nightly walk. She would have been with him when the driver slammed into her best friend. She had seen the worst; her mournful face told the story.

I was trying to muster up all my strength to make it through the next few days, years, yes, and the rest of my life as well. Afraid of what was coming and knowing Matthew would not be there as part of my support, grief swallowed me, ate my heart, and took me to a place that I had never visited before. The bottom of my soul.

Abandoned and lost, knowing that my son was gone, and my husband was slowly joining him in death–one piece at a time as his mind left his body—and there was nothing I could do to stop the bleakness of a future alone. I cradled my head in my shaking hands, leaned over the table, as tears flowed down and formed a puddle below. My despair lodged in my throat, and for a moment a cry emerged, so deep from a mother's broken heart, a sound so primal that it shook me. I pulled back my voice, weak yet with an ounce of hope, I implored, "Please God, how much more can I take? I need your help. I can't do this alone. Please help me."

I laid my head on the table, in the pool of tears, and pulled myself together. It took some time to gather my emotions, feel my heart, my breath, my soul being touched with a small bit of hope. I knew that somehow life would move on, and maybe God would help me along. Trusting in that, I sat up and gathered my emotions, my thoughts, my strength.

I remembered that last time Matthew was here with me, just days prior, when we indulged in a long and truly engaging conversation. Part of that discussion came flooding back to me as I recalled sharing with Matthew my idea about our souls never die, and should one of us die, we must promise to come and let the other person know--a sign that life continues beyond this earthly existence.

Recalling that specific request, that agreement we made to notify each other when one of us died, I got upset. "Damn it, Matthew, you did not come and give me that special sign. That was your promise. We had an agreement! Don't you remember that? You promised to give me a sign."

And then I remembered the miracle of that unimaginable evening the night before!

The tiny universe of sparkling lights, shining in front of me as I sat in the living room. Those beautiful little stars that were just within reach, yet not touchable. A field of energy that appeared three times, fading after each vision. This lovely array of lights exploded in front of me just after 7 pm, as we were waiting for the program to begin on the television. That is the time the detective told me that Matthew was killed.

Holy Cow! Those twinkling beautiful sparkling lights, those starlike wonderful little pinpoints of life, those were Matthew's sign! He did come! Matthew let me know he was okay! Why was I so blindsided by everything? He kept his promise. I was elated!

There it was, right in front of my eyes from that special night. I knew, that at the moment of his death, Matthew showed up as an energetic, spiritual being, a tiny galaxy of sparkling stars right there in front of me, in front of Sal, his energy emanating love and joy and life eternal! He was fulfilling his earlier promise, that whoever died first would come back and let the other person know all was well!

More than just bursting onto the scene, Matthew drew me towards that book about Edgar Cayce, *There is a River,* as if to say "Hey mom, you were right. I chose you and Pops as my parents. Look at the book. Everything is right there so you know what we were talking about."

The realization that Matthew had fully communicated with me was overwhelming. I have no idea how he learned to use his energy to create the thick storm of sparkling lights, so effortless, to prove he was still alive!

More than that, he honored me by evidencing validation that it was he who was guiding my focus. That's why he drew attention to the book which had been the basis of our discussion a few days earlier. I knew in my heart that my son was letting me know, at the moment he died, that all was well. All would be well. He promised to let me know he was fine after death; he knew I needed a spectacular sign, and wow, he did deliver. He passed his exam with flying colors!

Realizing that those lights were Matthew's sign, the book was just the icing on the cake. My son's ability to communicate after his death led me to open up and learn more about the afterlife. I wanted to delve into a deeper spiritual understanding about life, and my true nature, and connect with the spiritual world in ways I could not imagine possible. The sparkling lights the night Matthew died, combined with the Edgar Cayce book that had influenced my outlook on our pre-birth choices and family, and the knowing that my son had found a way to communicate with me immediately after crossing over— all influenced my decision to find a deeper meaning to my life.

I had pledged that once the next few days were over, after the services and whatever else needed to be done, when my life went into a new normal of my being here alone, caring for my husband, that I would start learning about Matthew's new world. Whatever knowledge that would bring would help me in my determination to care for Sal and keep going despite all odds. I knew that Matthew would be my guide, doing more from the spirit world than he could ever have conducted in his physical life. It took his death to bring back my life.

LIFE MOVING FORWARD

I knew in my heart the sparkly lights were a sign from my son, as maybe only a mother would understand. I truly believed that Matthew had survived his death. Not on this earth as a physical human, but as an eternal being, in spirit, moving about that ethereal and mysterious world. This acceptance that my son continued to live on in spirit gave me hope and inspiration, through the days of grieving and organizing, arranging, and keeping sane. As time moved beyond those first two weeks of pulling through, I could draw comfort in the belief that Matthew would always be there at my side, in spirit.

Life moving forward was complicated. My primary focus was taking care of Sal. His decline continued, and by mid-summer, he qualified for hospice care. This was so helpful—no more long trips to visit the doctors, as they came to the house. Nurses on a regular basis checked his status. Twice a week, the hospice caregiving staff sent someone to help bathe him. I hired a private caregiver to help one afternoon a week so that I could run errands and grocery shop.

Life at home after Matthew was not easy, but for the rest of that year I was able to manage whatever came my way regarding Sal. Lewy took over as Sal slipped deeper into the challenges of dementia. Stories abound about that situation, enough to fill a separate book.

The aftereffects of Matthew's passing were a different challenge. There was his renovation project sitting there needing attention, a house amid being remodeled. Some of the walls and ceiling had been stripped bare, awaiting fresh insulation and new sheetrock. The back yard had piles of construction materials--doors, pipes, windows and more--strewn about in haphazard fashion. There was a large storage room filled with tools, and more building materials; boxes of nails, screws, wiring, light fixtures, and on and on filled numerous shelves. His bedroom was full of his clothes and personal effects. How many shoes and pairs of socks can one person have? Furniture, appliances, housewares—this son of mine seemed to be the pied piper of any object he thought would be useful.

I was in over my head. In the good years of life, Sal, Matt, and I could tackle a project such as this huge task with no problem—clean and fix, replace and repair, organize and sell, make a few bucks, and move on. Not this time. It was just me. And my hands were full. I did not have the money to hire a crew to finish what Matthew had started so my best option was to sell the house as is. There would be little profit made, if any. A close friend of Matthew, Kevin, offered to help me sort through the mess and get the house ready to sell. No doubt Matthew had whispered in Kevin's ear to help me out, and I will always be grateful for his help over the coming weeks. Kevin not only helped clear out the house, and sell whatever could be sold, but he also spent some time helping me with Sal over those first two months after Matthew's death. I am forever indebted to his compassion and generosity.

Post death there is always paperwork—insurance, banks, financial dealings, and so much more. I was busy for a while. Matthew did not have much, but enough to keep me occupied with collecting and filing paperwork.

Delving into Matthew's papers, I discovered a job application. It was the one he had been working on, that day he had called me. That application to be hired as a part-time brewing assistant, the one he was filling out and asked for my input. The day he later died.

What jumped out on that application was something he wrote. There was a section on the form that said, "Additional training relevant to position applied for: (Please Explain)." Matthew wrote the most profound words. His response to what his training had been and what qualified him to be an assistant brewer, was as follows: "*Living & Loving Life All Day Every Day!*" Reading that phrase made a huge impact on me and has shaped my life moving forward. My kid, my incredibly interesting, crazy, and never quite settled down man—well, if that was his attitude on the day he died, who am I to not carry the thought in my life!

It took several weeks to sort through the details, papers, and belongings, to sell the house and car, and so much more. In between taking care of Sal, I was able to take care of Matthew's affairs, with one bit of unfinished business remaining: There was the criminal case of the driver who killed Matthew that needed some of my attention.

The day that a detective informed me that my son had been killed in a hit and run accident, the driver slamming him and not stopping, was one I will never forget. The news sinking in that this driver was so careless and heartless angered me. How could anyone hit another human being and not stop, care, or report? My heart went cold towards this unknown person, and I wanted revenge. Justice cried out and punishment surely would be duly imposed.

Weeks later, my heart softened, and those first feelings faded as I learned more about the person behind the wheel. The driver was a young man, in his teens, and his family had suffered their own share of tragedies and heartaches. He had no intentions of harming anyone that night; it was an unexpected yet terrible act, one he would have to live with. The police investigation and discovery led me to understand this driver was also a victim of that tragic night.

Almost a year after this hit and run, and the death of my son, the driver accepted a plea deal. I went to the sentencing proceeding and addressed the court, and in a sense, the driver. A very scared young man sat in the defendant's chair, with no family there to support him.

I read my statement, closing with "I, and my family and

friends, join Matthew in saying to the defendant, We forgive you. Now go and learn to live and love life, all day, every day!"

Those words lifted a heavy weight off my shoulders. The power of forgiveness was palpable. The defendant cried, the judge teared up, the courtroom became hushed as the sentence was read. The young man was given five years' probation. That was justice, done right.

Time to Reflect

Prior to Matthew's death, I had not given much thought to what one may experience when they reach those final moments in life, and what comes after. I had been walking this earth for over 60 years, and Matthew's was not the first death I had faced. My mother and grandparents had all passed, as had a few friends and other relatives. However, the search for a deeper understanding in the process they may have gone through had not inspired me to seek answers. I hoped there was an afterlife, a heaven for most all people, which would be pleasant enough to look forward to when the transition is made. I had heard that dead people can communicate with those left behind, but I was never interested enough to really pursue knowing more about after life communications.

The sparkling lights I experienced the night he died, that miracle sign I later realized were Matthew letting me know he was in another realm, made me curious to understand more about life after death. I began to consider the possibility that Matthew had not only communicated his continued existence that night, but that he could do so again. Somehow, someway, he could let me know he was hanging around—and maybe he could answer some lingering questions.

Visiting the park, standing at the base of the tree where Matthew's last breath was drawn and hearing what the neighbor experienced that fateful night made me wonder what it felt like, what Matthew went through in his transition.

A visit later to the funeral home, to sign papers and verify the body, was more heart wrenching than I had expected. His body had been so damaged, broken and battered, wrapped, and bundled so that only his face was available to view—contusions and evidence that his was not an easy death. The memory stirred up even more thoughts on what he felt in those final moments, the impact, the last breaths as he flew from the blow of an oncoming vehicle, his body coming to a rest when it slammed into the trunk of a tree. The horror of death.

I wondered whether, in the final few moments of my son's life, did Matthew have some pre-cognition his time on this earth was almost up? Why did he step onto that road, exposing himself to fate that night? He was a cautious person. Didn't he have an inkling the car that was approaching was going much too fast? What pushed him to ignore the danger and step across that road? Did he feel pain? Did he suffer from the impact? What did he see? What did he hear? What did he experience as he moved into the world beyond? Did he have a unique foreboding? Any sign that his life was about to change forever?

And what was going through his mind as those last breaths on earth took him out of his world and into the next? Was he alone, or was there a spiritual transition he experienced among angels or angelic spirit guides? What happened as he entered that cosmic realm of the afterlife, a world beyond anything I had ever glimpsed or caught sight of.

More importantly, how did Matthew send me those incandescent and shimmering lights at the very moment he transitioned? What other signs and communications were going to be made possible at a future date? How could I learn about these things?

The idea that he could communicate from the other side, could send me signs, intrigued me. It was all so new. I fostered a growing curiosity about the process of dying and wanted to know the details of whatever happens in the afterlife. This was my new path, my new quest. I was looking to nourish a desire for finding all the answers. It would take time.

Being a full- time caregiver for Sal involved a lot of personal time commitments and activities. Searching for answers gave me an outlet to keep me motivated beyond the daily commitments and routines. It took a while, but eventually, my questions were answered.

Matthew's affairs were settled, or close to being finished. Clothing, household goods, bits, and pieces of life not worth clinging to were given away or donated to a charity. A few items of memorabilia were shared with friends and family. I kept a few items, some with strong memories attached: a souvenir from a ball game, a vacation trip, an autographed trading card or two—those little mementos that describe his life, treasures to this day.

Caring for Sal could be time-consuming, but there were periods of quiet and calm. In those moments I could delve into my research of the afterlife and spirit communications. I perused the internet, ordered a number of books by a variety of psychics, mediums, and spiritual minded authors, and began my search for answers.

Answers from the Other Side

The descriptions on what happens after we humans cross from this physical existence into a spiritual dimension are consistent. A consensus that life is eternal, we are spiritual beings having a human experience, and love never dies was found in most of the material I read. These sources provided some more generic answers to my general questions, yet I wanted something specific, more personal to my connecting with Matthew.

Delving into a perspective about which I had little knowledge, learning that one can connect with those in the spirit realm, intrigued me. A hope began to emerge that perhaps a reading with a medium might serve as an avenue towards gaining insight, especially some answers as to why Matthew had to die when he did. Yet, I was a bit skeptical.

Years of watching movies and television programs in

which those who could connect with the dead were portrayed as maybe kooky, or scary, or dabbling into witchcraft had jaded my views. I knew that society in general seemed to scorn spirit communications, as did many religious beliefs. Yet, as I was reading these books, it seemed more and more plausible that those in the spirit world could and would be able to send us messages. After all, I believed Matthew sent me those incredible sparkly lights after he died. Surely, he could do even more.

My quest led to reading about spirit communications. I found several books describing mediumship, how the spirit loved ones can use a medium to connect with the mom, dad, or spouse left here on earth with grief and questions. Evidence that life continues beyond one's death was remarkable. Those who received validations and messages from their people on the other side were given hope, and in many cases, some healing in their grief. My skepticism began to diminish.

Three months after Matthew's death, I was ready to dive in and hear from my son. I set aside my analytical, and at times skeptical mind, and decided it was time to book a reading with a medium. I reviewed a website that had a lot of information and reviews on several professional mediums. After perusing the reviews, I passed over someone local, choosing instead a woman who lived on the east coast, one that was far away from my world. I sent an email requesting a session and was soon booked for a reading, by phone, with this medium.

Nervous and excited, I prepared for the scheduled session. I had my list of questions for Matthew, sure that he would be right there ready to reply. Soon, I would have proof that life continues beyond death and would discover why he put himself in danger. I had learned that one should not give the medium any details. Let them tell me who was here, and what the spirit has to say. Though sometimes a medium may need to clarify something, I was going to be very quiet for the most part.

The medium began our session, described how a reading works, set the expectations, and began connecting. Nothing more was asked of me at the beginning except my first name.

Well, to say the least, this was the best investment I had ever made in my life! This medium, knowing nothing but my name, connected with my mother first. She gave some details on mom's health, life, and how she died. Considering that mom had died over 25 years earlier, it was astonishing that this medium knew more about my mom than anyone outside of our close family. Wow!

The medium then described my mom bringing in someone, a young man. The description continued, his hair, looks, personality–all on target with Matthew. She did ask if I knew who this was, I replied: Yes. She then said that it felt like he was my son and asked if I had lost a son. I replied yes. And then we were off to the races!

Matthew was quite the communicator. She shared what he was telling her, showing her, his personality and unique laugh all came through. His dog and cat were with him. A friend who had died a few years earlier was also there, the medium describing her quite clearly. Matthew had to work on detailing his passing, but soon he was clearly giving the information I needed.

His description about the circumstances of his death was remarkably transformative. Matthew shared that he was trying to go from one side to the other, but instead of reaching the other side, he went to the other side. The angels were there to meet him. They told him it was time to go, to cross over, and he went with them. No pain, no fear. It all happened so fast, but the angels took him and led him home. At one point he remembered looking down at his body, life barely holding on. An angel asked if he wanted to stay, and he was shown his life moving forward, if he remained here. He decided that the road to recovery was too much for him, and for me, who already had a commitment to aid Sal, so he chose to go with the angel.

Matthew relayed to the medium that he was more concerned about me, and said he was sending love from his side of life. He let her know that he had sent me lights when he died, a sign that he was okay.

This was what I really needed to hear. The medium had much more to say; all of it was more than I could have hoped for. Matthew finished with a little encouragement for me moving forward, including an assurance that my life would get better. A hope for the future to carry me forward.

The medium shared that Matthew was concerned about my feeling lost, not knowing how to begin. He told her that the day would come when I would be helping others, be of service, and learn about spirit communications. He also said that someone would be coming into my life, a mentor, a person I would be working with in service to others and that I would be happy again.

I was relieved to know that he had angels with him, and that he was meant to cross over to the other side, not reach the other side of the street. No, instead he crossed over and reached the other side of life. That world of heaven and love and ancestors who have gone before. And he was keeping watch over me! And of course, those little lights were him, how could I ever doubt?

This reading with the medium got my attention. Matthew admitted to sending me those lights that night he died, and I knew there was more. This miracle of life, not as an apparition, but as an energetic phenomenon, was the first of numerous signs that my son's life continued after his transition.

I was puzzled by his prediction that I would be working again; being retired and taking care of Sal at that time, my going back to a job was far from my future plans, but those closing comments got my attention. It would take time for them to become reality, and they would do so in a most remarkable way!

LOOK FOR THE SIGNS

The morning after Matthew's death, when I drove down the road, not knowing that my son had transitioned, there was that flock of bluebirds that crossed my path. Spirit has a way, and somehow, Matthew influenced those birds to catch my attention. It was even more remarkable in that bluebirds are rare in my area, especially in the winter.

Watching those birds fly skyward, I remembered Matthew as a toddler. He loved to sing a song with the lyrics about Mr. Bluebird on my shoulder. That happy memory brought a smile to my face as I continued down a dusty road. Before reaching home, another song popped in, "Over the Rainbow" from the *Wizard of Oz*. I could hear that well- known song with the part about "where bluebirds fly" playing over and over in my head as I returned. Bluebirds and rainbows, whenever those signs or images or words appear in my life, I am drawn back to that morning drive, memories of Matthew, moments before I heard he had crossed into the world of spirit.

Months later, I experienced a very sad morning: my first Christmas without Matthew. I rose that day feeling down and wishing he was near. A noise outside my window drew my focus to look outside. There were several little bluebirds in the berry bush; they were merrily chomping on the little red treats. Amazing! Seeing those little feathery friends felt like a special gift from my son and were a perfect present on Christmas day. Realizing what was happening, I addressed Matthew directly: "Thanks Matthew, this is beautiful!" One blue bird paused and glanced towards the window. It felt like he was looking directly into my eyes. I clearly heard my son's voice say, "You're welcome!", as if he was standing right there with me! Let me tell you, that brightened my entire day!

Over the years since Matthew crossed, bluebirds continue to remind me that he is near, watching over me. There are numerous occasions where I will think about Matthew, a memory pops in, I come across a photo or a reminder of his life, step outside and there is a bluebird, sometimes a flock of them, out in the yard. They have been showing up more often, each winter it seems the gathering of blue feathered friends is more and more frequent and getting larger as time moves on— from a rarity to a more common sighting, always reminding me of that one special morning drive.

During the months that I was writing this book the bluebirds seemed to be more of a presence in my area. I would spend hours writing and re-writing pages, go outside to get some fresh air, and there would be a flock hanging out in the trees in my yard. I would send my editor the latest version of the manuscript, take a walk to clear my head, and a bluebird would be flitting back and forth across the road in front of me. One day, I was in a phone conversation with my editor, discussing some changes to my book. She suddenly gasped, and said, "You won't believe this, but as I looked outside just now, there are bluebirds sitting in the juniper tree outside. I have never seen bluebirds here before!"

I find it interesting that at my home, which sits on several acres of juniper-woodland in northern Arizona, surrounded by a lot of trees, the bluebirds typically hang around the front area near the garage where Matthew's classic pickup truck is stored, and the area just outside my bedroom window. I never see them in the back yard, nor along the far edges of the property. Almost as if they just want to be near his truck and near my bedroom window.

Rainbows are a theme, another connection to Matthew, and to this day are a very welcome sign. I know that my son is not the one creating them, but I do think he encourages me to notice them at the exact moment when they appear. Since his passing, the rainbows keep popping up, not only as a sign for myself, but also for others who were in his life. I began to write down in a journal every time a rainbow would show up. Often, they pop up in unexpected ways, moments after I was beginning to think of Matthew. Rainbows tend to appear and can come as lovely reflections following a storm, or as prisms reflecting from a glass or from sunbeam. Rainbows have come in with mentions in books, or social media posts, in song lyrics on the radio, also in conversations with others, and in so many other amazing ways. My son is truly somewhere, over a rainbow, within a prism of color, in a song lyric or a special photo that catches my eye.

Rainbows are often interpreted as signs from loved ones. Often, I have read posts on social media, especially in the Helping Parents Heal group, of loved ones and rainbows. The song "Somewhere over the Rainbow" is often a reminder that our children and other loved ones are far above, in a heavenly realm.

I began to associate Matthew with rainbows shortly after he crossed. As I was pulling out photos to use for his celebration of life video, one in particular stood out. Two years earlier, we had been sitting outside after a nice summer rainstorm. Matthew was standing in front of me talking, and I noticed a rainbow appear just behind him. I pulled out my camera and he posed, as if he was holding that rainbow up with his arms outstretched, hands cradling the colorful arc. This photo became the theme of his memorial. One of his friends made a large copy of this photo, framed it, and gave it to me as a lovely gift. They added the words "Our little Ray of Sunshine," a nice tribute.

This theme of rainbows has also come up in other remarkable ways, often unexpectedly. In the years since Matthew crossed, I have had the opportunity to delve deeper into spirit communications and messages. There have been classes, presentations, and development groups that I have been involved in to learn about how to connect with loved ones. Often, Matthew has communicated with several fellow students and developing mediums in a variety of settings, and he has come through with rainbow imagery on a number of occasions.

One day, in a practice session, one of the students connected with Matthew. He was showing her that he was wrapped in a rainbow blanket, surrounded by other young men who had also crossed over. She said, "Matthew is with several young men in spirit, they were lining up and he was helping them so they could provide messages to their moms."

In another practice session, a mediumship student described the following: "Matthew has messages for you. He is going to inspire your spiritual growth and is a guide helping you reach a turning point. He is excited that you are finding ways to connect with him, to continue being a part of each other's existence. Matthew is showing life going from a darkness then transforming into a beautiful rainbow, representing the changes coming in your life."

One remarkable weekend of Matthew and rainbows stands out. I had been involved for several months with a small online development group. We were practicing our ability to connect with spirit, honing our mediumship skills. The opportunity to meet in person at a weekend retreat, focused on a small group of budding mediums, presented itself, and three of us decided to participate.

In our circle a few days prior to this weekend gathering, Matthew connected with one of the group members and said that rainbows would be a theme for the coming weekend.

We pondered this message and were a bit curious as to how he was going to bring us rainbows. The gathering was going to be held in Phoenix, a hot dry desert, and no rain was in the forecast for the coming days. Well, he did not disappoint.

The person Matthew gave this message about rainbows to resided in the Midwest and had to fly to Phoenix one very frigid morning to attend the weekend program. She was startled at one point when looking out the window, sitting on the tip of the wing, was a circular rainbow! Feeling Matthew laughing at this, she grabbed her phone and snapped a photo. A very unusual phenomenon—yet there was a rainbow to start off that weekend gathering.

The first afternoon of our weekend experience with several other developing mediums, the facilitator arranged for us to gather in a circle and prepared to play a recording to settle us into a meditative state. The music that started playing was not the expected quiet, transcendental type of song one would expect. Nope. Instead, the "Over the Rainbow" played. So, Matthew again found a way to work a rainbow into our weekend.

Later that same afternoon, the facilitator offered us a little break. She opened her freezer and pulled out popsicles for anyone interested. Not just any popsicle, but Rainbow Bomb popsicles. Not only did we get the rainbow once again, but earlier that day, as we sat together and connected with loved ones as a group, Matthew communicated with some of the students. At one point a student sensed Matthew with a bluebird on his shoulder. Another student heard him say he was "Da Bomb."

So here we are later in the day, enjoying rainbow bomb popsicles. What are the odds?

That evening, my fellow friend and student opened up her text messages on the phone. She laughed and shared with us some messages, and photos, from her grand-daughter: drawings of rainbows. Yep, another rainbow connection.

That weekend as Matthew predicted, there were rainbows–one on the tip of a plane, a song, a popsicle, and a drawing from a child. He even threw in a bluebird just for fun. The ways of spirit to get our attention are ever amazing!

One day a fellow student in mediumship texted me with a photo. She had just asked her device to play 70's gold music. Instead, it played "Over the Rainbow/What a Wonderful World," and she heard Matthew say, "tell my mom I said hi."

In 2017, I attended a small group reading at the home of a medium in the Phoenix area. At one point in her demonstration and connecting with loved ones, she heard the song "Somewhere Over the Rainbow," looked at me, and said "Your son is here."

Matthew has shown me more than rainbows to grab my attention. There are multiple ways he lets me know he is around. One of his specialties involves playing with the ceiling fans. There are two fans that he installed in the kitchen and dining area. I have lost track of the number of times he has turned on those fans or allowed the lights to flicker. This often happens when I am in the room talking on the phone with his girlfriend Alex, or when someone is visiting, and we are spending time talking in the kitchen, sharing stories of you know who.

Once, I was working on a little decorative project, refinishing a frame around a mirror, and wondered if the mirror had been from Matthew's house, one that I had kept after we cleaned out the place. I no sooner had the thought, and the ceiling fan kicked on. No doubt this happened to validate my thought that yes, this was Matthew's mirror.

Matthew also demonstrates his abilities whenever we have family gatherings at the house. We might all be sitting down to dinner, and when someone mentions the fact that Matthew would love something about the gathering or a certain story that is being shared, almost on command, the lights turn on and both fans start whirling. "Hello Matthew!" That's what we all say.

When those fans and lights move, clearly, they do not turn on, not at random. Not coincidentally. They only do so if Matthew is being discussed, or thought of, and only on occasion. I am convinced he can play with those, no problem.

Matthew has communicated in other interesting ways. One night a few weeks after he died, I woke to someone knocking on the front door. I got up, opened it, and no one was there. No one. I live in a rural area, with a very long driveway. No one out there. Days later, I experienced another wake-up call. This time there were seven raps on my bedroom window. To my surprise, again, no one was there.

One of his best friends, Kevin, called me one evening, and was ecstatic. "Diane, you won't believe this, but I found my name written on the driveway at Matt's house! It was written in big letters in oil! He sent me a message! He wrote my name in the driveway, how the heck did he do that?" Kevin had been at the house helping clean it up and getting it ready to sell. He had moved an oil pan that was sitting on the driveway, probably placed there weeks earlier under Matthew's old truck which leaked oil. To his surprise, when he picked it up, the letters "KEV" were written, in oil, on the concrete. I can't explain that one, but there it was, the name was clear as could be, and spelled out on the driveway.

Many people report seeing their loved ones in spirit. I have not yet experienced seeing Matthew, but I am convinced one night his dog, Abby, saw him. My stepdaughter Patricia and I were sitting in the living room, going through photos, trying to put together a memorial program. Abby was lying in the corner, snoring. Suddenly she perked up, we heard her dog tags clinking and looked at her. Abby was transfixed on something, as if there were someone standing in front of her.

She stared and stood up and seemed to follow an imaginary being as it moved across the room, in front of us, and towards the door. Abby headed to the door, as if there was someone there, walked up to it, and stared for a few moments. Patricia whispered, "I think Abby sees Matthew." I replied, "I think so, too. Just look at how focused she is."

Finally, Abby relaxed and glanced over at us, as if to ask, "did you see Matthew too?" I had no doubt. Dogs are more attuned to spirit energies, so she probably did see him cross the room that night. You can blot out the point of many events, or you can open your eyes and choose to see what the true significance of events are all about.

My stepson, Guillermo, had a more remarkable appearance. He called me one morning to tell me "I saw Matthew last night! I was starting to go to sleep; suddenly, I felt someone next to my bed. I opened my eyes and saw Matthew, as if he were standing right there next to my bed. I could only see him from the waist up, but he was right there, like he was fine. I told him that I was so sad that he had died, and I said, "I am so sorry." Matthew then spoke to me, he said "I forgive you." A moment later, he faded away."

When Guillermo told me this story, I had no doubt that Matthew had come to visit him. They had a very strained relationship over the years, for very valid reasons. Guillermo had been a challenging person in Matthew's life, to put it mildly. Guillermo may have had some unresolved guilt about the past, and I believe it was very plausible that Matthew would find a way to come to him and offer forgiveness. This was powerful. For each of them.

There were a few people that shared with me stories of hearing from Matthew, maybe catching a glimpse of him, or a dream. I recall my dad saying that Matthew showed up at his house; he saw him sitting on the couch one night a few days after Matthew died, they even had a short conversation. A cousin said she saw Matthew show up in her kitchen, heard his laugh, but just for a few seconds. She called his name, and he disappeared. Alex, Matthew's girlfriend felt Matthew wake her up one day, shaking her to get up and get going. There are many tales to share, all of them quite amazing.

There were moments for me when a special song would start to play, one that reminded me of Matthew. Such songs would play at random, maybe at a store, the car radio, or a restaurant. I would turn on the radio and there would be a special song, a moment of connecting with him. One song in particular caught my attention, because it was important to Matthew. Following his death, I found a notebook in his truck. In it he had noted the title of a song "I Will Wait" by Mumford and Sons, a recently popular song on the charts. That for me was a song to his heart. Of course, Matthew is over there on the other side, waiting for me, waiting for Alex, waiting for all his friends and relatives. I still tear up when that one starts playing, wherever I am.

My favorite stories though came from Sal. His dementia continued to be a growing concern over time, but I think the condition permitted him to connect very closely with the world of spirit. There were many times when he would relate that Matthew had been by for a visit. On multiple occasions, Sal related words to the effect: "Matthew was here and said hello" and "Matthew and my mom came to see me and to visit this morning."

This statement interested me since Sal's mom had died many years before I had even met him. So, for her to be coming to him with Matthew at her side seemed significant.

One day, Sal amplified what had been happening between Matthew and him. On that day, Sal related the following: "Matthew told me that when I die, do not be afraid, he will be there to help me." Later, Sal added: "Matthew told me that he is getting pretty good at helping people who are dying." Well, I felt that statement was really uplifting and remarkable!

On occasion, I would hear Sal talking to someone, a would-be unseen visitor. "Who are you talking to?" I would ask. Sal would come up with a ready reply: "Matthew. I was telling him to take care of the dogs" or "Matthew was asking about my life in Mexico." There were several different discussions they seemed to be engaged in. I was a bit jealous, as I never had the chance of hearing Matthew talking to me so openly like that.

There are so many signs and messages that I have received from Matthew, some to remind me that he is around, others to nudge me along my spiritual path. Matthew has been quite adamant that I write down his story, this book. Over the course of the past several years, he has communicated this imperative, to share my experiences and tell others how life continues, and our loved ones are always right there.

For example, in a group reading for a special online presentation by one established medium making connections, Matthew stepped forward with the following message: " I don't know if you do a lot of writing, but I see that there's some writing from this child that is very spiritually attuned, that the words could help others, so you need to write, and give some kudos back!"

One of the lovely students I have studied with, one who is now a practicing medium, has also connected several times with Matthew. For well over a year, shortly before covid struck, she would call me and share that my son had communicated with her the importance of my writing a book, to share his story with others.

A year ago, I had still not started to write Matthew's story. I attended a conference and met a couple of interesting women, fell into a good discussion about spiritual matters, and exchanged contact information. Two weeks later, one of the women called me. "Your son has been telling me you need to write his book. He says it is time." Well, that was a surprise. A woman I barely met two weeks earlier, who to the best of my knowledge was not a medium, but an author, a poet, a retired educator was telling me that my son is nudging her to get me working on his book. More than just a nudge, she offered her assistance in editing this book, as she had the skills and experience as an editor. Well, with that big push I had little choice but to start this book, which you are now reading. Good job, Matthew!

These are just a small sample of what I continue to attribute to Matthew's new reality and continued presence in our lives. There were so many more opportunities for spirit communication; in fact, there continue to be more amazing connections from Matthew in my life.

Even now, and up to this very day, I often still hear from friends, or family. Matthew had come to someone in a dream, or a few family members thought they heard his laugh. When they began thinking of him, suddenly a rainbow would appear. He finds a way to drop in when least expected.

EYES OF GRIEF

Three years after Matthew's transition, my perspectives on life, the afterlife, and the world of spirit had transformed me from one who had doubts, into one who knew that there is a heavenly place, a home away from this crazy and challenging earthly existence. His death led me to a journey of learning, discovery, understanding and acceptance.

Death certainly has a way of changing us. Sal succumbed to dementia two years after Matthew's transition. The awareness that he would be fine, that his soul would join Matthew's in their new spirit home amplified the knowledge that they would both watch over me. The fact that I could feel their presence, and one day would join them, helped me move forward.

Four years prior to Matthew's death, I received a phone call from a dear friend. One of the few people I knew and had kept a friendship with, since my days before Sal and Matthew were in my life. Her voice shook, and through tears and sobs, she told me that her eldest daughter unexpectedly, tragically had died.

A few moments of silence were shared, I had no words to say, and my friend needed to catch her breath. I did not know how to help, what to do, where to go to help my friend. Death of a child, one who was part of my extended sense of family, had never entered my world, and I was no help.

Years later, she was the first friend I contacted after I received the terrible call on Matthew's death. Our families had been close, and Matthew sometimes referred to her as his other mother. Her daughters referred to my son as their little brother. She knew my heart, and listened to my tears, and we shared a few moments of silence. My friend knew what had to be done. Through tears and shock, she was able to help, guiding me with what I needed to get through the next steps. She knew.

As I was finishing this story, this book, I received a phone call. Another friend and mother. She was one who shared my quest for further spiritual understanding and development. We attended workshops and many discussion groups together. We had been engaged in delving into the deeper meaning of life. She had supported me through my son's death, and later, the death of my husband.

My friend's voice shook, her son had also met a tragic death. The details were not shared, not that important. My friend had called me, and I knew. Days later, I was able to meet with her face to face, at a candlelight service for her son. When we met, we hugged, and hugged, and cried, and pulled back and looked into each other's eyes. No words. Our hearts knew what only those who have lost their children knew, and we hugged some more.

My friends and I were not alone.

WHERE LOVE NEVER DIES

After Matthew's death I was led to a group of people who had gone through what I had gone through. These were parents who had lost their children and were looking to find connections and answers. Helping Parents Heal (HPH) was a growing organization. It had originated in Phoenix a few years prior, and members of this group were just what I needed at that time.

These parents would get together, bond, and then begin sharing stories of their children, the heartbreak, the shock, the grief, the love. They accepted that their children were now in heaven. Those same children were sending love, supplying signs and messages. They knew that there is and always will be a path along which to move forward. One will never completely recover from the loss of a child, but life can look a little brighter over time.

Every parent who is new to this group is looking for their child, the love of their life, the beautiful human who is no longer here in this earthly realm. The perfect soul who is missing from the perfect life. Meanwhile, nothing is perfect for anyone. Everyone shares some measure of sadness and grief, sometimes so debilitating that one cannot see the light, the path to move forward. Each grieving parent is earnestly looking for the evidence, the validation, and the proof that love can and will not ever die. Helping Parents Heal offers a place to find that comfort.

At the time following Matthew's death, I needed support from others who knew of my grief. Whenever possible, I planned for Guillermo to come and keep an eye on Sal so that I could go to Phoenix and attend one of the group monthly meetings. I could not go every month, but when the opportunity presented, I made sure to attend.

During each gathering, there were guest speakers. I especially looked forward to the presenters who were well-known mediums, practicing professionals who had volunteered to help the parents meet the spirit of their beautiful children. The survival of consciousness, the forever love that binds child to parent, these are the essential elements that can move one from deep grief to a place of hope and a degree of healing.

The abilities of these mediums to connect parents with their children with amazing evidence, stories of loss and love was incredible, astonishing, and undeniable. There was a way to make people's lives much better. Healing was available when it was least expected.

One medium was highly regarded and instrumental for the group at the start up. She would meet at least once each year with the parents to share evidence from the children. Her presentations were always packed. I attended two of her demonstrations for the group; one time the room was so packed I had to sit out in the hall and strain to hear her. Both times, this medium made amazing and heartwarming connections with the children in spirit and their parents in the audience.

Every time I attended a gathering with any medium making connections, providing evidence that our children are near and dear, I prayed that my son would come through, with something, anything. In these wonderful heartwarming moments, when parents heard from their children, I would be excited for them. Meanwhile, for myself, Matthew was quiet in these gatherings, not a peep. I was disappointed, especially knowing what a social outgoing person he had been in life. He was not hesitant to pop up with signs, playing with ceiling fans and other interesting ways of getting noticed. Yet, he was reticent to speak out in these larger gatherings. I was beginning to wonder if Matthew had begun to lose interest in communicating with me.

A PREDICTION

Time moved on. Three years had passed since my son left this physical world and entered a whole new existence. He had sent signs along the way. Inspired to delve more deeply into learning about Matthew, and later Sal's spiritual dimension, I found my way into a number of books, workshops, and conferences about the afterlife and communications from the world of spirit. I became acquainted with a group of other parents who were on a similar path as my own, finding support and compassion.

And yet, with all I was learning, and accepting, and knowing that our people in spirit are always nearby, I was still a bit lost. My future was unclear. Days and weeks were passing and life was really challenging—and boring. I was sitting at home most of the time, with no real idea on how to engage with others beyond my little circle of family and friends, most of whom lived far away. I was afraid that maybe my loneliness, if shared too often, would make them not too eager to converse with me. I mean, how many people want to hear about your loss and difficulties adjusting? I imagined not too many.

Occasionally, to keep my memory fresh, I would listen to the recording of the reading I had with the medium a few months after Matthew's passing. It was uplifting to hear her describe Matthew, and his dog, and his messages. I would feel a bit better being reminded that he had been wrapped in the arms of the angels, that it was time to go. Most of the messaging was encouraging, and helpful. Yet there was one section that had me puzzled every time I heard it. It was a prediction about my future, and it had not yet come to pass. It was clear, yet a bit cryptic.

One cold winter's day, I am sitting around feeling sorry for my losses, lost in a world of pity and inertia, wondering how I was supposed to move forward when all seemed so forlorn. I decided to replay the recording, and as usual, it helped me feel connected with my son. I listened intently to his message about my future, and pondered when, or how this was going to come to pass. Here is what was communicated in that reading that puzzled me:

"There is a lot of discussion taking place about you starting over—about you feeling very lost—not really knowing how to begin. He keeps talking about how you will be helping younger people, being of service, and that you are going to continue to learn about spirit communication.

"They have another person that's been really close to you in your heart, but that you went in a different direction. They keep talking about you becoming close to someone but they're working on their business. This

is a new person that is going to be coming into your life, a mentor. I think it is somebody you are going to be busy helping others with, and it pertains to the business. They are putting the business in order right now. You're going to be happy again. There is a whole another life coming for you. You are meant to have a good life, and to be of service. A lot of people with different needs will be helped by your service."

Listening to these words, one more time, I could not fathom how in the world this could ever come true. Who is this person that is "really close" to me, working on a business, coming into my life as a mentor? Me, helping others, being of service, a new way of life is coming? I just could not understand how this could happen. Maybe if I got off my couch and volunteered with a community service organization? I just did not have the impetus to move beyond my little home of feeling sorry for myself, so this prediction was going to be a miracle should it ever come to pass.

I have heard it said that miracles happen. The universe seems to open, and everything falls into place, as though it was all planned out ahead of time. When all seems to be at a dead end and life seems pointless, when you think there is nothing left and all hope has vanished, when thoughts of giving up start to dance about in one's head, that maybe it is time to ask for help. All it takes is a prayer, from one's lips to God's ears.

I sat there that sad day, with the memories and longing to move out of my sadness and loneliness and prayed. I asked God for help. I asked for my life to change for the better. I needed a small miracle to keep going. I hoped God was listening.

New Beginning

For nearly three years, Matthew had been quite good at sending signs that he was alive and well in another dimension, but in early 2017 he had been rather quiet. I was beginning to worry, "Was he busy over there in heaven? Has he moved on to something more interesting than watching over my life? Has he forgotten me?" I wondered if the relative tranquility in my quiet surroundings had bored him. If so, I hoped he was off on some exciting adventure in his world of unlimited boundaries.

Matthew tended to show off when there were guests in my home. Playing around with the lights, the ceiling fans, the television to make his presence known, but over the recent holiday season there had been no visitors at my home, no festivities, not much going on in my world. Matthew may have been having a good time of it, but I was in a rut. Nowhere to go, nothing to do that inspired me.

Most of my life I helped care for my younger siblings, followed by my own family—husband, son, and stepchildren. Decades of active involvement in their lives. I had finally reached a stage where I was not involved in caring for someone else, and adjustment took time. I really did not know what to do with all that time on my hands. Matthew had been gone three years; Sal had passed the year before. For the first time in my life, I was not immersed in taking care of anyone but myself. Some days I had trouble just doing that.

Despite my supplications to God for a small miracle, a prayer I had whispered earlier in the week, here I was again on a lonely afternoon, holding hands with inertia. Living in this house, filled with the memories of better times, could be emotionally overwhelming. Family photos, memorabilia, years of creating a home, could at times weigh down my emotions, and tears would roll. I really needed something to motivate, inspire, and move out of the stagnation that had set in—either that, or just give up and wait out my turn to leave this dreary place and join my guys over there in their new world.

Sitting there that lonely afternoon, feeling stuck in a quagmire of my pity party and disconnection from life—both here in the physical and there in the afterlife—I recalled my prayer to God days before, hopeful that my prayer would be answered, yet getting a bit impatient as days moved on.

In my sad little state of mind, feeling alone and in some ways, wishing I could just give up, the phone rang. Startled, I jumped at the unexpected noise and picked up the phone. The caller ID showed a name, a person I recognized. The previous year I had attended several workshops and presentations from a known spiritual teacher and medium. On Mother's Day the previous year she had provided a mediumship reading for me, connecting me with both Sal and Matthew. Though I knew her through her professional work, it seemed strange that she would be calling me out of the blue.

"Hmm, why is she calling me? Maybe Matthew has something to say" I wondered. I mean, miracles do happen, right?

Excited now at the prospect of a message from my son, I answered "Hello" with a slight nervousness in my voice. The response was not what I had expected.

"Hi Diane! I am calling to ask if you are interested in a job prospect." Well, that threw me off. She continued to explain that a colleague of hers had contacted her to see if she knew anyone who wanted a part-time work at home type of job. Someone who may have some interest and knowledge about mediumship. She said my name popped up in her mind, and recalling my interest and studies in the field, thought maybe I would be interested.

Well, that caught my attention!

She gave the name of her colleague who was looking for a helper, and I was even more surprised. This was the medium that I had seen at a recent Helping Parents Heal meeting. In fact, it was the very first medium I had considered contacting for a reading following Matthew's death, three years prior. I really liked her at first glance of her website but did not make contact, mainly because I thought it may be better to find a medium who did not live in Arizona, one who would not have any connection to the area, as Matthew's death was broadcast in Phoenix news outlets. I did, however, feel a certain draw to this local medium, even if I did not reach out to her. So here I was, three years later, being asked if I would be interested in working for this person. What are the odds of that happening?

I knew at once that Matthew had a hand in this arrangement. He may not have made a peep when I saw this medium connecting other parents with their children, but he sure knew how to communicate when it was something really big!

No doubt Matthew was tired of seeing his mom sitting around the house feeling lost, and rudderless. My son had been eavesdropping, heard this medium needed a helper, figured his mom was the perfect fit, and made sure my name was mentioned when the time was right.

The possibility of working for this medium was beyond my hopes, and not something that I ever considered would happen. Hey, I was retired, with a lot of time on my hands, but had not seriously considered working again. Yet here was a great opportunity. "Of course!" I replied, trying not to sound too eager, yet inside my heart was bouncing up and down and ready to explode.

A little later this medium called to discuss the opportunity. She shared with me her story of reaching out to her colleague to inquire if she knew anyone knowledgeable and interested in part time work, for a medium. Her tale proved that Matthew was the instigator!

She said that finding someone who could understand

the work and was available and interested was not an easy quest. She called her friend and relayed her hopes in finding the right person. As she hung up, the ceiling fan in her living room kicked on, full blast! Surprised, she and her husband both looked at the whirling fan, then down at the remote sitting on a table, and back at the fan. "How the heck did that happen?" they wondered. She sensed that spirit was playing around and knew that the right person would be found.

I was elated at her telling of the ceiling fan, and excitedly shared, "That would be my son, Matthew. He plays with the ceiling fans in my house. He set this up!"

She responded "Okay, let me check here....yes, I have your son. He is laughing, and standing next to you, his hand on your shoulder, and saying "yes" he is the culprit."

Well, what a great start to what has become a very good working relationship, and opportunities to learn, grow and understand the world of spirit—all thanks to Matthew!

Matthew blew open a door and pushed me through into a whole new way of life! He orchestrated the circumstances, creating a connection that altered my path. He arranged that the right people, at the right time, would reach out to me when I most needed a purpose, a plan, a reason to keep on going. The message in that earlier medium reading, the prediction that I would be entering a new phase in life, was coming true!

Not only that, but God was listening! This prospect, this offer, to work for a highly regarded medium was a miracle! Even more incredible, I have been led on an unexpected adventure, a deeper exploration of the afterlife, mediumship, and spirit communications under the mentorship of this incredible person.

Working for this medium has afforded me the opportunity to expand my knowledge about the world of spiritual communications and the afterlife. With her mentorship, I am learning how to connect individuals with their loved ones in spirit. This is not something I felt I was "born with," but an ability I could tap into through hard work, focus, practice, and engagement to develop that "sixth sense," that ability to feel, hear, and see those in the spirit world—to share their messages that love lives forever with their loved ones here, still on the physical plane.

I went from a seeker, hoping to connect with my son in spirit, to being able to connect others, as a medium, to their loved ones on the other side of the veil—truly being of service to Spirit!

Since I started working in this new direction, I have had numerous and incredibly fascinating experiences to share. I participated in several classes with other students learning mediumship, sat with them in development circles and practice. My fellow students often connected with my son, and Sal, and some of my other family members in spirit. I too made connections with their spirit people. As a developing medium I also practiced with volunteers, people I knew nothing about, and was able to feel, hear, sense and relay messages and evidence that love never dies from their loved ones. So many stories to tell, I hope to share my experiences and the process of mediumship in a future book: *Finding the Medium Within*.

For now, I hope you have felt the tragedy and grief, the sorrows and the joys, the hopes, and the healing in our story. Matthew arrived in my life as an unexpected gift, a beautiful little angel. I know, every parent feels this unconditional love when holding their baby. Thus is the joy of life. We hold their tiny hands and guide them through the road of life. No matter how long that journey, there is an unbreakable bond.

Matthew was my son. His life was filled with love, adventure, some drama and challenges, some good times and some bad. Like most of us, he had his struggles, but always managed to pull himself up and get going again. Through it all, he was a good son, friend to many, mentor to some. His unexpected death hit hard. I have mourned, cried my heart out, cradled his special teddy bear, worn his favorite cap, yearned to hear him laugh one more time. Yet, I know he is well. After all, he keeps sending me signs from his life on the other side, reminding me that he is always here, and sometimes, when I sit in silence, I can feel him near me, his essence infuses my soul, and I hear him, laughing once again.

I have a purpose, a love for the future. I needed that, and Matthew brought me that world. The sun is shining in my life, and it gets brighter every day—all arranged by my Matthew, my forever gift from God!

I leave you with a parting thought. No matter the challenges, the adventures, the hardships in my life, I always fall back to the words my son wrote, the last day he walked this Earth. His interpretation on why he was well suited for a job to brew beer, a phrase which I carry in my heart and recall when life gets a bit overwhelming, and I need a boost.

I call up Matthew's Mantra. I hear his voice, his laugh and his words, and everything feels a little bit better:

"Living & Loving Life All Day Every Day!"

The End

ACKNOWLEDGMENTS

I thank all the wonderful family, friends and so many others for their encouragement, advice, and support, without whom those early days of tragedy would have been so much more difficult. In the years that followed, these wonderful souls were instrumental in making Matthew's story become a reality.

First and foremost, I want to acknowledge my son Matthew. This story began with him, the journey was carried forward with his inspiration and nudges, and the tale closes with his inspiring words.

Matthew left this physical world in January 2014. Years have passed since he walked over to the Other Side. In this time, he let me know he was fine, and he made sure to nudge me, over and over, to write down this story. I lost track on how often he reached out to me, directly, and through others, to share this remarkable journey with you, the reader.

Thank you to my family and closest friends who were there for me when the struggle to keep going was real: Stephanie McCann, Alison Kittle, Patricia Calderon Massingill, Guillermo Calderon, Alexandra Perkins, Anasztaizia Morgan, Teresa Perkins, Buena Redick, Jesse Horton, Bill & Laura Fields, Margaret Mendoza, Brenda Robbins, Mary Rose Wilcox, and Kevin Bourgeois.

I am especially grateful that Matthew opened my circle of connections to other parents on their own journey through grief and wisdom, to fellow students developing their intuition and mediumship and to those teachers and mediums who encouraged and helped my development in understanding, communicating with and connecting with those in spirit.

My special warm thanks to those fellow parents who have shared their children in spirit, and given their support over time, especially Elizabeth Veney Boisson, Lisa Wilcoxson, Laurie Savoie, Elizabeth West, Colleen Smith, Tracy Soussi, Brian Smith, Dolores Salazar Cruz, and Claudia Milligan.

To those in the world of intuition, mediumship, development, and interest in all things spiritual I have a special place in my heart. A portion of my journey included readings from evidential mediums, those professionals who I had the pleasure of experiencing messages from Matthew, and sometimes Sal, my parents, and others of my loved ones in spirit. In gratitude for the healing: Cheryl Ann McGill, Suzanne Giesemann, Susanne Wilson, Fara Gibson, Jamie Clark, Mark Christopher Nelson, and Debra Martin.

Many of my new circle of fellow students and soul tribe helped this story move forward, providing suggestions and inspiration, so a special thank you to my soul sisters Brenda Bollman Baker, Lynette Setzcorn, Jayne Howell, Valerie Kwietniak, Raven Maestas Valencia, Sandy Thorpe, Suzie Myers, Mary Hauprich, Karen Morrissey, Britta Grubin, and Nina Cree.

Also thank you to my fellow travelers in learning about spirit, who also helped provide guidance and insight in this production: Joy Collins, Terry Angell, Donna Bell, Chris Wolever, Diana Suchoff, Mary Berry Kurrasch, and Gary Langley.

No book will ever reach publication without the guidance of editors, reviewers, and coaches who can make things happen! Elizabeth Martina Bishop, PhD contacted me a few days after I first met her at a spiritual conference in Los Angeles. She relayed that my son Matthew had been nudging her to reach out to me, he wanted his story made public. It just so happened that Elizabeth had some abilities to connect with spirit, and she had experience over many years as an editor. Well, I could not ignore the extension of this help, so with her guidance, Matthew's story emerged.

My next step towards publication was to connect with Joseph M. Higgins, who is a medium, and an established author and coach/mentor on self-publishing in the genre. Through his expert guidance this story has become a published book. Without his expertise and gentle advice, I would have been lost in the world of publishing.

And finally, a very special note of gratitude to my mentor and greatest supporter in my journey from grief to transformation, Susanne J. Wilson, the Carefree Medium. It is she whom I first considered contacting for my first ever medium reading, but instead I chose someone else. It was Susanne who was looking for an assistant, and Matthew made sure to connect us. Through her mentorship, guidance, and patience, Susanne drew me into her world of spirit communications. I moved from a novice in this arena to a seasoned student of mediumship, through practice, practice, practice—to becoming a certified medium under her tutelage. We have collaborated over the past several years, and for that I am forever grateful that Matthew brought us together.

AUTHOR PROFILE

Diane Calderon graduated from Arizona State University with a Master's degree in Sociology, and served in various levels of government throughout her 30+ year career, including Postal Clerk, Community Organizer, Job Developer, Contracts Specialist, Research Statistician, Union President, and Deputy Director of the Governor's Office of Affirmative Action.

Following her career, she retired to enjoy time with her family in rural northern Arizona. Life had other ideas. Diane became a full-time caregiver for her husband as he traveled down the challenging road of Lewy Body Dementia. Amid caregiving, her only child, Matthew, died in a tragic accident.

Incredibly, Matthew began to communicate from the Other Side, sending signs and messages that love never dies. His continued presence sent Diane on a new trajectory, helping her move forward from the grief of losing both her son and soon after, her husband. Delving into studies in spirituality, survival of consciousness, after death communication, and mediumship, inspired by Matthew, has led her on a new path in life.

Diane authored an article for *Psychic News Magazine* and was featured in a documentary "Life to Afterlife: I want to talk to the Dead" on Amazon Prime. She has completed certification for Reiki Master and Mediumship.

Diane is currently working as a Client Services Manager for Susanne Wilson the Carefree Medium. She can be contacted at dianecalderon46@gmail.com or on her webpage wwww.DianeCalderon.com

Resources

Helping Parents Heal
Helping Parents Heal is a non-profit organization dedicated to assisting bereaved parents.
https://www.helpingparentsheal.org/
https://linktr.ee/helpingparentsheal

Open to Hope ®
Open to Hope is a non-profit with the mission of helping people find hope after loss.
https://www.opentohope.com/

Made in the USA
Middletown, DE
08 September 2023

37782730R00096